Adam to Abraham

An Internet-Linked Unit Study

About the Author

Robin Sampson

Robin Sampson is a homeschooling mother of eleven, grandmother of twelve, and author of several acclaimed books including *Ancient History: Adam to Messiah*, *What Your Child Needs to Know When*, *A Family Guide to the Biblical Holidays*, *Wisdom: An Internet-Linked Unit Study*, and *The Heart of Wisdom Teaching Approach*. She is a contributing author to *Things We Wish We'd Known* and *Lab Science: The How, Why, What, Who, N' Where Book*.

Robin actively lives her subject as she continues to home-educate her youngest children. Several of Robin's children are grown, married, and homeschooling their own children. Robin's husband, Ronnie, is an assistant deputy director for Homeland Security in Washington, D.C. They reside in northern Virginia.

William Dennis Ward

William Ward contributed to several lessons in this book. William holds a B.A. in pastoral studies and biblical theology and is also educated in electrical engineering. Along with a career in the computer industry, he has written and co-authored a number of Bible studies and serves as an elder in his home church in Mariposa, California. He is the author of *Shall He Find Faith*.

Adam to Abraham

An Internet-Linked Unit Study

BY ROBIN SAMPSON

Contributing Author: William Dennis Ward

Heart of Wisdom Publishing
http://HeartofWisdom.com

Disclaimer

Heart of Wisdom is nondenominational, functioning entirely apart from any denominational agenda. The main objective of our unit studies focuses on students and parents learning God's Word and establishing a relationship with Him. The listed resources and links are provided as a service. Opinions and materials contained therein are those of the individual ministries and/or authors and may or may not reflect this author's position on particular issues. Many scholars with varying doctrinal opinions are able to contribute to specific areas of research. This book includes research or recommended resources by Christians of several different denominations and by Jews, Messianic, fundamentalists, etc., in cases in which it is evident that their area of expertise is correct in investigating the truth. This does not mean that the author or publisher is in doctrinal agreement with authors of contributed scholarly text or of recommended resources.

Copyright May 2001
Revised and expanded July 2003
Heart of Wisdom Publishing
Woodbridge, VA. All rights reserved.
Web site: http://HeartofWisdom.com
E-mail: Info@HeartofWisdom.com

Printed in the United States of America

No portion of this publication may be reproduced in any form, electronic or otherwise, for any purpose other than personal (family) use, without the author's express written permission.

Adam to Abraham
An Internet-Linked Unit Study

Table of Contents

Key to Symbols 6

Interacting with the Internet 7

Unit Overview

    Adam to Abraham Overview 10

    Adam to Abraham Objectives 12

    Scheduling and Teacher Helps 13

    Adam to Abraham Vocabulary 18

    Adam to Abraham Time Line 19

    Adam to Abraham Resources 20

Lessons

    Introduction .25

    Creation 30

    Garden of Eden 36

    Adam and Eve 39

    The Fall 44

    Cain and Abel 50

    Seth to Noah .54

    Corruption of Man 57

    The Flood 61

    After the Flood 66

    The Tower of Babel 71

    Beginning of Nations 76

    The Nations' Religions 82

    The Calling of Abram 86

    Abram Enters Canaan 93

    Genesis Reveals the Messiah 101

Back Matter

    Paper People 108

This unit takes a historical look at Creation. Heart of Wisdom's book, *Creation: An Internet-Linked Unit Study*, examines creation and evolution theories in depth.

Adam to Abraham

Key to Symbols

Resource Symbols

 Book or magazine

 Internet site

 Audio resource

 Resource suitable for all ages (read-aloud)

 Key resource

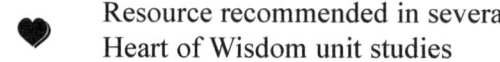 Resource recommended in several Heart of Wisdom unit studies

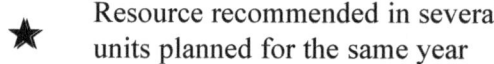 Resource recommended in several units planned for the same year

♦ Resource recommended in several lessons in a unit

 Video or television program

Activity Symbols

 Writing assignment

 Vocabulary or list

 Copy passages; outline; fill in a worksheet

 Listen

 Map work

 Create artwork

 Contrast and compare

 Add to Time Line Book, make a chart, or make a graphic organizer

 Expand research

 Think and discuss

 Write a letter

 Prepare a meal or recipe

 Experiment

An Internet-Linked Unit Study

Interacting with the Internet

The Internet is an open door to an enormous, exciting library. The wealth of information on the Internet can be overwhelming because a search for a single topic can lead to thousands of links; but Heart of Wisdom units guide you to the best and most appropriate Web sites to enhance each lesson. You can go quickly to the links from **http://Homeschool-Books.com.**

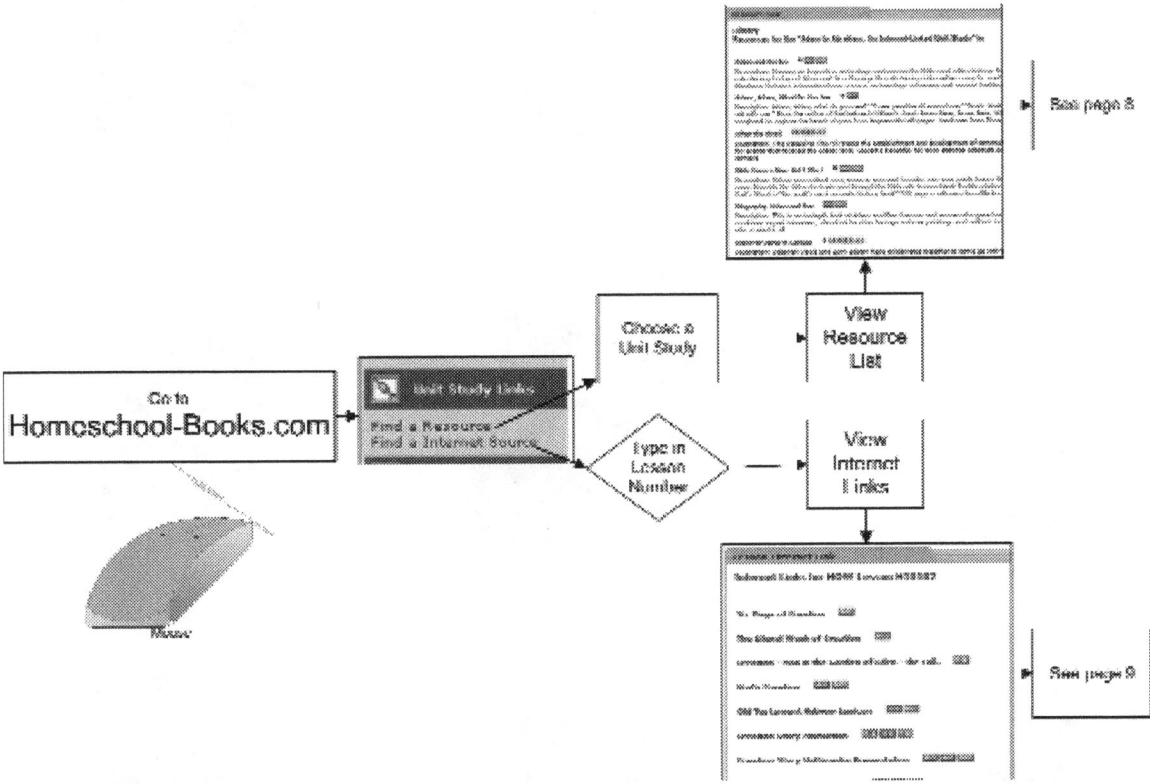

To access the links, you will need

- A PC with Windows 95 or higher, or a Macintosh PowerPC/Power Mac with Mac OS 8 or higher;
- A browser such as Internet Explorer (IE) or Netscape (we recommend IE);
- A connection to the Internet by either modem or cable;
- An account with an Internet Service Provider (such as AOL or MSN);
- For some content, you may need a "plug-in" (such as RealPlayer, QuickTime, or Shockwave, which allow you to play audio or video files). There is usually a button that allows you to download any necessary plug-in(s) at no charge.

Recommended in: ♦ several lessons in a unit; ★ several units in a volume; ♥ several volumes. ☞ Key Resource for this unit.

Heart of Wisdom Publishing

Adam to Abraham

Resources Listed by Thematic Unit Study

When unit studies first became popular in the homeschool market, resource suggestions were a big problem. Many times the resources were hard to find or out of print. Our Internet links solve this irritating problem. Go to http://Homeschool-Books.com and click on FIND A RESOURCE. Simply click on the link to go to the online vendor carrying the product. Alternative books are listed for any books that go out of print. The resources on our site are listed alphabetically and marked by grade level K-3 4-8 9-12.

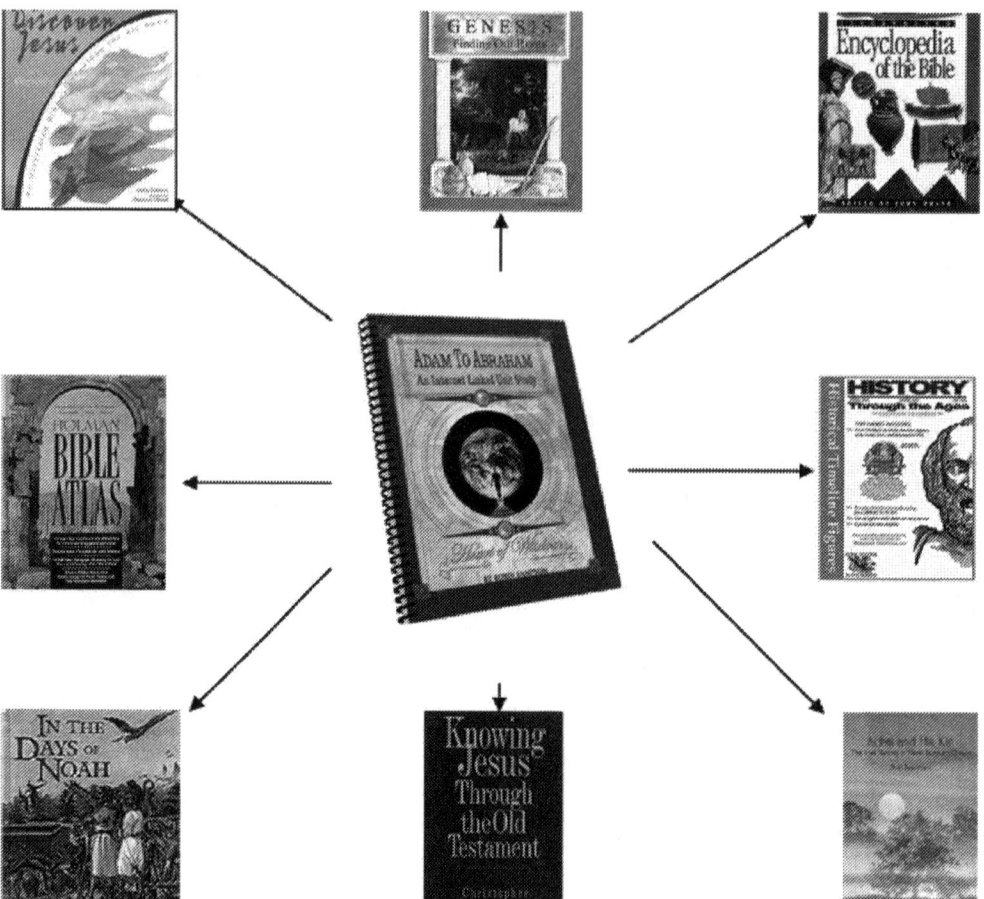

About the Resources

The suggested resources are completely optional. This unit study includes so many links to information on the Internet you can use this unit without refering to any additional resources. However, students need to read (and feel and smell) real books! We have included several resources that are popular with homeschoolers so you can utilize what you have on hand. You are going to make two investments in your homeschool: time and money. Investing in good resources will save time. Utilizing the library and inter-library loan will save money. Each family will need to consider the resources they need based on their homeschool budget, time available, the number of children that will be using this program, and their personal interests.

This book was written for grades 4-12 but we included resources for younger children to benefit families with several ages. If you are using this book with younger children, the lessons will require reading aloud and simplified explanations for the younger grades.

An Internet-Linked Unit Study

Internet Links Listed by Lesson

Links are available to maps, articles, Bible studies, video clips, photos, audio files, worksheets, instructions, interactive lessons, etc., which are appropriate sites for a given lesson. To access the proper links, go to http://Homeschool-Books.com and click on *Find An Internet Source* under the *Unit Study Links* menu. Type in the Lesson Code (example: H10102) to view the links. Sites are marked by appropriate age level K-3 4-8 9-12. Sites that include worksheets are marked with a pencil.

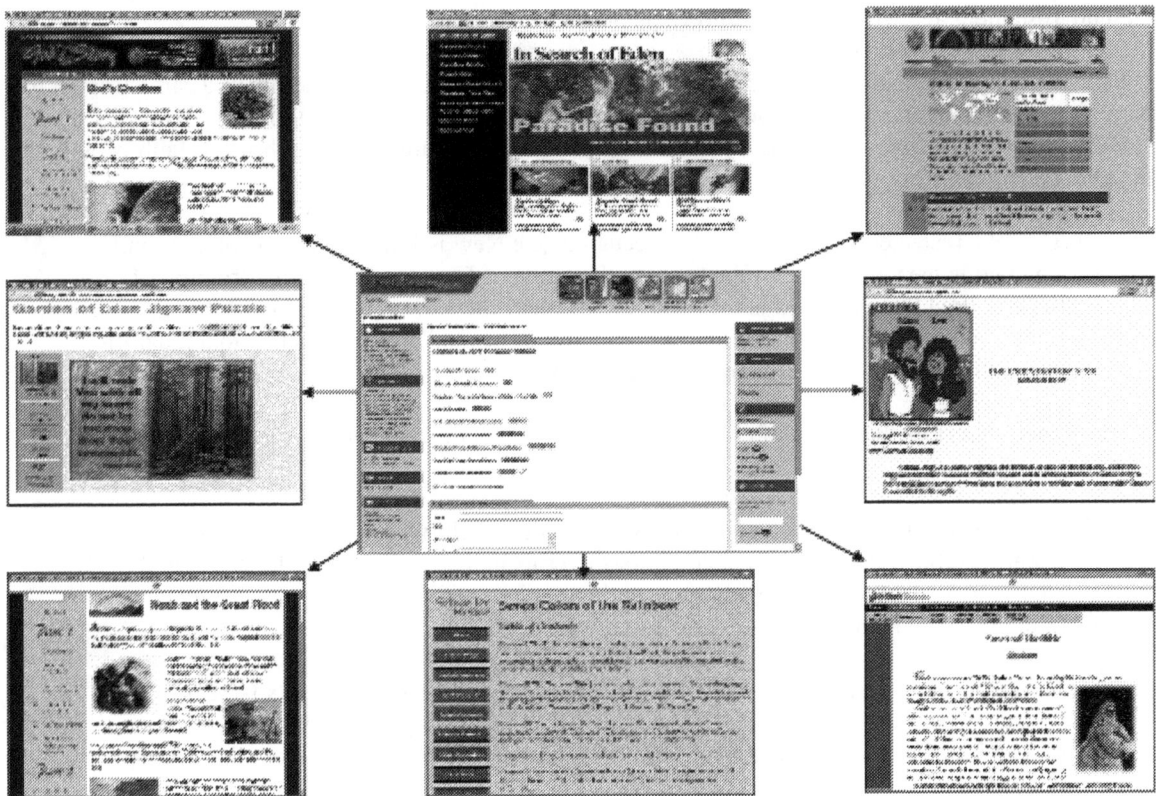

Internet Safety

The computer can be a wonderful tool, but also a great temptation. We suggest that you view all sites with your children or, at a minimum, have your computer in an easily seen area in your home (never in a child's room or turned away from parental eyes). Typing in long URLs can mistakenly lead to undesirable sites. We recommend that you use **http://Homeschool-Books.com.** to go directly to the applicable sites and avoid typing in URLs.

Site Availability

URLs for Internet sites change, and sometimes sites go offline completely. HOW links are continually updated with new links, new resources, and alternatives to dead links. Occasionally, you may get a message that a site is down. This usually means that the server is busy and you can try again later.

Recommended in: ♦ several lessons in a unit; ★ several units in a volume; ♥ several volumes. ⊙— Key Resource for this unit.

Adam to Abraham

Adam to Abraham Overview

Except for a few familiar passages—Genesis 1, Psalm 23, Isaiah 53—The Old Testament remains a closed book to most Christians. Yet it was the only form of Scripture which was used by Jesus Christ, the Apostles, and the first Christian community. Jesus referred to the Old Testament consistently. When the words were written, *All scripture is inspired by God and is useful for teaching, for reproof, for correction, and for training in righteousness* (1 Timothy 3:16), the statement was referring to what we call the Old Testament and what was then known as Scripture.

Old Testament stories and prophecies laid the foundation for understanding the life of Jesus Christ in the New Testament. We cannot fully know about Christ and His purpose for coming into our world without studying the Old Testament gives us a picture of Christ's sacrifice for sin. The Christian faith is built on the Old Testament. Erich Sauer, in his book *The Dawn of World Redemption*, said this:

> The Old Testament is promise and expectation; the New is fulfillment and completion. The Old is the marshaling of the hosts to the battle of God; the New is the triumph of the crucified One. The Old is the dawn of morning; the New is the rising sun and the light of eternal day. If Christianity, the "religion of Christ," may be likened to a magnificent cathedral, the Old Testament is its unshakable foundation.

David Egner, describes the riches of the Old Testament in the book *Knowing God through the Old Testament*:

> The Old Testament story emerges like a tiny shaft of light way off in the distance, races toward us through the darkness, and bursts over us in a crescendo of light, color, and sound. It fills our minds, our emotions and our spirits with the majesty and presence of Almighty God Himself.
>
> It's a marvelous story as it unfolds. It's Adam's story. It's Noah's story. It's Israel's story. It's our story. But most of all, it's God's story. It's the opening of His book, the explanation of His character, and the record of His mighty deeds among men from the beginning of time.
>
> The Old Testament is a book of great spiritual and personal value because it tells us about God:
>
> - It answers questions about how life began.
>
> - It tells how evil came into our world.
>
> - It prophesies of the Messiah-Redeemer.
>
> - It inspires us to holy living.
>
> - It fills our hearts with gratitude and praise.

The Book of Genesis is the book of origins. The word *genesis* (Hebrew *b'resheet*) comes from a Greek word that means origin, source, or beginning. The first eleven chapters of Genesis begin with Creation and the first man and woman, and move to the seventy nations of the world which are called "The Table of Nations" in Genesis chapter 10. Genesis chapters 12–50 comprise the ancestral story. The focus of this unit study is on Genesis 1–12, with a brief introduction to the call of Abram (God later changed Abram's name to Abraham) and the Promised Land. (The culture of the Mesopotamian world of Abraham is covered in the *Mesopotamia* Unit Study, and the Hebrews' ancestral story is told in detail in the *Ancient Israel* Unit Study.)

The stories in Genesis chapters 1–12 include the divine act that brought humanity and history into existence and enabled humanity to exist, multiply, diversify, and disperse upon the earth. It is the story of how God created a world that was good but which becomes corrupted by sin, which enters the world through human disobedience. Adam and Eve ate fruit which was forbidden to them, and Cain murdered his brother Abel. God later commanded Noah to build an ark in which pairs of all living things were preserved from the great Flood which God sent to purge the earth. God set the rainbow as a remembrance of His covenant with Noah. Afterward, people began building a tower that would reach to heaven in order to make a name for themselves, but God confused their speech and scattered them. Then God again appointed a man—Abram—with whom to establish His covenant.

The messages taught in Genesis are taught throughout the rest of the Bible:

  1. God is sovereign. (Above or superior to all, greatest, supreme)
  2. God has a plan which He is carrying out.
  3. God is able to take the evil and cause it to serve His eternal purposes, thus bringing great good out of it all.

The entire Bible finds its meaning and explanation in the redemption provided by Jesus Christ. Each lesson in this book reveals shadows and types of the great doctrine of salvation by grace through faith in the death and resurrection of Christ. As you teach your children about the Creator of the universe—the story of the Fall, of corruption, the Flood, the call of Abram—remind them that God takes control of every situation in our lives. He is the One who commands the wind and the waves, and He is the One who knows us by name. He is the One we can call on at any time.

Footnotes

1. Sauer, Erich. *The Dawn of World Redemption: A Survey of the History of Salvation in the Old Testament.* Paternoster; 2nd edition (1985) ISBN: 085364411X. <http://www.worldinvisible.com/library/sauer/dawnredm/dwrtable.htm>
2. Sper, David. *Knowing God Through The Old Testament.* RBC Ministries (1990) Grand Rapids, MI <http://www.gospelcom.net/rbc/ds/sb101/>

Recommended in: ♦ several lessons in a unit; ★ several units in a volume; ● several volumes. ☞ Key Resource for this unit.

# Scheduling and Teacher Helps

Pray for guidance as you plan your schedule. Only God knows the needs of your individual child. The time you spend on each lesson will depend on the level of your student(s), your resources, and the activities you choose. There are sixteen lessons in this book; you can complete one lesson a day for a three week study or expand the lessons over several weeks or months. Remember your main goal is in Matthew 6:33, *"Seek ye first the kingdom of God, and His righteousness, and all these things shall be added unto you."* There are four steps in each lesson, and you should touch on each step in each lesson. The average time for each step is:

- **Step 1:** Five to ten minutes to discuss the lesson.
- **Step 2:** Thirty minutes to an hour to research and read sections in the resources (several hours for high school students, or longer if the student is extremely interested in the subject).
- **Step 3:** Thirty minutes to two hours to complete each assignment or project.
- **Step 4:** Up to an hour to correct and share work (or ten to twenty minutes if only sharing).

Important: Do not skim or skip Step 1. This step baits the hook in order to catch the fish. It activates prior knowledge, creates interest, generates focus, and whets appetites. It is an essential anticipatory set with direct relevance to the instructional objectives that secures the attention and interest of the learner. This step engages the student by relating the material to his or her own life and experiences. Studies show that 70% of children do not do well beginning with Step 2, as traditional schools do by diving right into a subject. Step 1 establishes continuity with previous lessons, finds out what a child already knows about the topic, transmits learning expectations, and makes the new material relevant.

One of the best ways for a student to understand a topic is to write or talk about it. Using these processes, students will comprehend the material, restructure the new information, and then share their new understanding. Writing and narrating assignments are both about learning and creating new ideas. In each lesson during Steps 3 and 4, younger students should be able to tell you in a few sentences (narration) what the lesson was about. You can write down the narration to include in the students' portfolio. Older students should either copy passages, or complete writing assignments. During these assignments, students learn how to assess information and determine its appropriateness, how to evaluate and compare, analyze and discern, add their own feelings, organize information, and communicate conclusions. Students develop excellence in achievement by producing the required quality assignments; they develop diligence by continually practicing clarity, accuracy, relevance, prioritizing, consistency, depth and breadth through writing activities. They retain the material longer and practice writing mechanics at the same time.

Essential Teacher Helps
For more details about the Heart of Wisdom Teaching Approach, instructions for creating various notebooks, guidelines for correcting written work and worksheets, go to our Internet site at http://Heartofwisdom.com/Helps.htm or see our book *The Heart of Wisdom Teaching Approach*, soon to be available from http://Homeschool-Books.com.

See these Files Online
at http://HeartofWisdom.com/Teacherhelps.htm

- Bible First Philosophy
- Delight-Directed Studies
- Charlotte Mason Methods
- Learning Styles and the 4 Steps
- Writing to Learn
- Correcting Written Work
- Multi-Level Teaching

- Creating a Portfolio
- Creating a Time Line Book
- Creating a Vocabulary Notebook
- Creating a Spelling Notebook
- Graphic Organizers
- Worksheets

*This book was originally written for grades 4-12. It has been revised to include activities (Step 3) and resources (Step 2) for grades K-3; however many of the lessons will require reading aloud and simplified explanations for the younger grades.

An Internet-Linked Unit Study

Adam to Abraham Objectives

Objectives are listed by lesson. Objectives with an asterisk (*) are intended for grades 9-12. Upon completion of this unit your student should:

All Grades, All Lessons

- Gain a closer relationship with God through the study of His Word.
- Develop an appreciation for the world God has created.
- Be able to use various Bible study tools such as a Bible dictionary, Bible encyclopedia, Bible atlas, concordance and/or lexicon.
- Be able to plan and conduct simple research using reference materials such as the dictionary, encyclopedia, atlas, thesaurus, Internet, and other resources.
- Be able to use data to construct reasonable explanations.
- Be able to communicate investigations and explanations.
- Be able to present results in a variety of ways, such as orally, in writing, and in other forms, including models, diagrams, and demonstrations.
- Be able to define, label, and demonstrate the Vocabulary Words (page 18).
- Demonstrate organizational skills using a portfolio or notebook system.
- Develop listening skills in order to follow oral directions, take notes from lectures, etc.
- Review sequence, fact and opinion, inference, and predicting to enhance his or her ability to develop critical note-taking skills.
- Be able to review topic, main idea, and supporting details to enhance ability to develop critical note-taking skills.
- Be able to construct an outline from various resources.
- Be able to organize information in several graphic organizers such as Venn diagrams, time lines, and charts.
- Be able to list proper citations in written work. *

Introduction Lesson

- Know the major sections into which the Bible is organized as a key to understanding the Bible.
- Have a firm foundation for this unit study through familiarity with Genesis chapters 1–11. The fall of man (1-3), his subsequent wickedness and judgment in the flood (6-9), his universal rebellion as evidenced at the Tower of Babel (10-11:9), and Abraham's call after the dispersion of the nations in 11:1-10.
- Know the major events and key people from Genesis chapters 1–11, and use this information to create a Time Line Book which will be added to throughout this unit study.
- Be able to explain the major sections of the Old and New Testament.*

Recommended in: ♦ several lessons in a unit; ★ several units in a volume; ♥ several volumes. ⌕ Key Resource for this unit.

Heart of Wisdom Publishing

Creation Lesson

- Understand that the Creation took place in a series of six days that were the same as the days of twenty-four hours which we now experience.
- Understand and appreciate the truth of Creation as opposed to ancient creation myths and modern-day evolutionary beliefs.
- Be able to tell the story of the Creation.
- Appreciate how the Creation reveals God.
- Know two Hebrew names for God.
- Know that Jesus was with God at the Creation.
- Understand that God created each of us for a reason, out of love.
- Have a feeling of gratitude for the glory and wonder of God's creation.

Garden of Eden Lesson

- Be able to imagine what the Garden of Eden was like.
- Understand that the Garden of Eden was too beautiful for us to fully imagine.
- Understand God will again create for us a perfect environment, in the future, like that of the Garden of Eden, that we can enjoy if we believe and trust in Him and His Son.

Adam and Eve Lesson

- Appreciate how wondrous it is that of all creatures, God created human beings in His own image.
- Understand Adam was assigned caretaker over all the earth (Gen 1:28).
- Know the Hebrew words for *Adam* and *Eve*, and understand the significance of their meanings.
- Be able to explain how God created Eve, and why the way in which she was created is important.
- Know why Jesus is referred to as the *Last Adam*.*
- Understand that Adam's rule was a picture of Jesus' rule over all creation when He returns as King (Rev 5:10). *

The Fall Lesson

- Understand the effect that sin had—and has—on mankind.
- Be able to imagine the sadness God must have felt when Adam and Eve, His beloved children, sinned against Him.
- Know that God still loved Adam and Eve even after they had sinned.
- Understand that all human beings sin, and that sin keeps us separated from God, just as Adam and Eve were punished for their sin by being separated from God.
- Understand that temptation can lead to sin if we allow it to do so.
- Be able to discuss ways of dealing with temptation.
- Understand that our debt to God for our sins has been paid in full by Jesus.
- Be able to tell the story of the Fall and its consequences.

Corruption of Man Lesson

- Understand the subtle way in which Satan led Adam and Eve to sin.
- Understand the subtleties of the sinful nature.
- Understand the effect that sin had and has on both mankind and creation.
- Know that all sickness and disease come from the corruption caused by sin.
- Be able to describe antediluvian society and culture.*
- Know that, according to Jesus, the days before the Flood characterize the days just before His return.*
- Understand what "corrupt" means in relationship to the nature of man.*

The Flood

- Understand the condition of man led to the Flood.
- Understand Noah's obedience and commitment to God in building the Ark amid the criticism he received.
- Understand that sin touches every generation and must be punished.
- Realize that Noah's Flood was worldwide and extinguished all human and animal life except for the lives of those in the Ark.
- Appreciate the Flood and its effect on the earth.
- Understand how Noah's protection from the Flood was a sign of a Christian's protection from death. *

After the Flood

- Describe the physical changes in the earth after the Flood.
- Know that Noah's first act upon exiting the ark was to build an altar of sacrifice.
- Understand, in general, how civilization spread over the earth after the Flood.
- Understand how both God's wrath and mercy can be seen in the Flood.
- Understand how the rainbow was a sign of God's promise.
- Understand the concept of making and keeping promises.
- Know what is meant by the term "Noachide laws."*
- Be able to name the seven Laws of Noah.*
- Understand the importance of the Noachide Laws and the effect these Laws have on society.*
- Understand how the idea of law is used in the Bible.*

The Tower of Babel

- Consider possible reasons why Noah's great-grandson, Nimrod, had no fear of God.
- Know about the development of city-states in Mesopotamia.
- Know about the construction of ziggurats.
- Know about the pagan religion created by Nimrod and his subsequent building of the Tower of Babel.*

Adam to Abraham

- Grasp the story of the Tower of Babel and explain its effect on today's world.*
- Understand the establishment of Nimrod's empire, Babylonian, and his relationship to various legends.*

Beginnings of Nations

- Understand that all peoples are descended from Noah and his three sons.
- Know the three primary races of the world as described by anthropologists.
- Know from where the word *Semitic* comes and to whom it refers.
- Understand the racial, linguistic, and political divisions of the genealogy of nations.
- Understand the term *Table of Nations*.*

The Nations' Religions

- Understand there are many world religions.
- Understand approximate geographic dispersion of world religions.
- Be familiar with the generations from Noah to Abram.
- Grasp how to determine the length of time from Creation to the Flood.
- Understand the importance and vital role faith played in the lives of Noah and Abram.
- Know the five primary world religions and approximate statistics.*
- Know the races coming from each of Noah's sons and where they settled.*
- Grasp that the religions of nations evolved from the perversion of the truth, and they all attempt to answer fundamental questions.*

The Calling of Abram

- Be able to trace Abram's travels from Ur to Canaan.
- Know that Abram followed the call of God; first an implied call, then a second and more definite call. He followed without knowing where he would be led.
- Grasp the effect the history of Abram had on the ancient world, and has on the contemporary world.
- Understand the relationship between Abram's call, his obedience, and God's redemptive plan.

Abram Enters Canaan

- Understand the land (later known as Israel) and people of Canaan.
- Be able to trace the migration of the Canaanites from their original home.
- Be able to trace the borders of the land of Israel.
- Be able to locate Israel on a map or globe.
- Be familiar with the surrounding areas of Israel.
- Know the land of Canaan, given to Abram by God, was renamed Israel by the Lord.
- Understand the history of the term Palestine and how it is used today.

An Internet-Linked Unit Study

- Have a general understanding of the physical characteristics of Israel (e.g., landforms, bodies of water, soil, vegetation, weather and climate).
- Use materials to make a model of a Israel that shows its physical characteristics (e.g., landforms, bodies of water, etc.).

Genesis Reveals the Messiah

- Understand that the Old Testament Scriptures are full of exciting stories of God's promises and grace though symbols and illustrations of Christ.
- Know the prophecies given in the Book of Genesis that foretell the coming of the Messiah.
- Understand that there are types that portray the Messiah in Genesis.
- Understand the Old Testament is an outline of God's design for Israel lived out in the story of Jesus. *
- Understand the Jesus was involved at Creation. *
- Understand the historical facts about Adam that illustrate Jesus.*
- Understand the blood sacrifice made after the Fall was a foreshadow of Christ dying for sin.*
- Understand the meaning of Jesus the Last Adam.*
- Understand that the historical facts about Noah, the Flood, the Ark, and the rainbow promise foreshadows salvation through Christ.*
- Understand that the Messiah is born from the seed of Abraham. *
- Understand the faith of Abraham is a picture of salvation. *

Recommended in: ♦ several lessons in a unit; ★ several units in a volume; ● several volumes. ☛ Key Resource for this unit.

Adam to Abraham Vocabulary

See Vocabulary Instructions.

A.D.	descendant	primeval story
ancestor	Divine Council	primogeniture
animal husbandry	Eden	Promised Land
antediluvian	ethnic	Pseudepigrapha
antiquity	Eve	rebellion
babble	Fall	repentance
Babel	Fertile Crescent	Sabbath
banish	Flood	Table of Nations
B.C.	forefathers	Torah
Canaan	genealogy	Tower of Babel
catastrophic	lineage	utopia
C.E.	metallurgy	vagabond
cosmology	myth	ziggurat
covenant	nation	
Creation	Noah	God (names)
		Adonai
		Elohim
		El Shaddai
cubit	origins	YHVH
		Hakadosh Baruch Hu
		Ribono shel Olam
deluge	Pentateuch	Harachaman
		Avinu Shebashamayim

An Internet-Linked Unit Study

Adam to Abraham Time Line

Approx. Time	Person	Years Lived
Creation c. 5500 B.C.	Adam (Gen. 1 & 2; 5:5)	930
	Seth (Gen. 5:3; 5:8)	912
	Enos (Gen. 5:6; 5:11)	905
	Cainan (Gen. 5:9; 5:14)	910
	Mahalaleel (Gen. 5:12; 5:17)	895
	Jared (Gen. 5:15; 5:20)	962
	Enoch (Gen. 5:18; 5:23)	365
	Methuselah (Gen. 5:21; 5:27)	969
	Lamech (Gen. 5:25; 5:31)	777
The Flood c. 3113 B.C.	Noah (Gen. 5:28; 9:29)	950?
	Shem (Gen. 5:32; 11:11)	600?
	Arphaxad (Gen. 11:10; 11:13)	438
	Salah (Gen. 11:12; 11:15)	433
	Eber (Gen. 11:14; 11:17)	464
	Peleg (Gen. 11:16; 11:19)	239
	Reu (Gen. 11:18; 11:21)	239
	Serug (Gen. 11:20; 11:23)	230
	Nahor (Gen. 11:22; 11:25)	148
	Terah (Gen. 11:24; 11:32)	205
c. 1775 B.C.	Abraham's Migration	175

Recommended in: ♦ several lessons in a unit; ★ several units in a volume; ♥ several volumes. ⚬— Key Resource for this unit.

Heart of Wisdom Publishing

Adam to Abraham Resources

The resources listed here are entirely optional and provided merely for your convenience. The resources suggested are considered the best of the best—homeschool favorites—therefore, we have included them in the lessons with reading suggestions, indicating page numbers, to enhance and increase your instruction. A very important part of teaching your child to love to learn is making available interesting resources. It is also enormously valuable to demonstrate essential study skills such as pulling together information from several different resources, particularly when researching Bible topics.

Resources with a ☞ are the most pertinent resources for this unit study. Resources with a ♦ would be useful in several lessons in this unit study. Resources with a ★ are suggested in several units done during the same year. Resources with a ♥ are suggested in several Heart of Wisdom Unit Studies. This study was designed for grades 4–12; however, we have included resources for all grade levels to accommodate families with children of all ages. Approximate grade levels are indicated with the following symbols: K-3 4-8 9-12 . Resources are listed alphabetically.

Resources Suggested for This Unit

Adam and His Kin: The Lost History of Their Lives and Times by Ruth Beechick ♦ 4-8 9-12

Description: Drawing on linguistics, archaeology, astronomy, the Bible, and other history, Dr. Ruth Beechick writes an enlightening and entertaining history of Adam and his offspring. An engaging, enjoyable, informative, easy-to-read account of Genesis from Creation to Abraham. Includes information from science and ancient traditions. Paperback (1991). Arrow Press; ISBN: 0940319071.

Amazing Expedition Bible by Mary Hollingsworth ♥ K-3 4-8

Now, children can discover not only what happened, but when it happened, and what else was happening at the same time in this collection of 60 of the most significant Bible stories and events retold in chronological order for children ages 8 to 12. This helpful resource is packed with sidebars and inserts of important and/or fun historical events that parallel the Bible stores in time. Other features include "history mysteries" and "Bible mysteries," which offer solutions to baffling questions. A full-color illustrated Time Line helps kids keep track of what else was going on in the course of history. Fascinating, full-color graphics, illustrated Bible maps, plus an alphabetical index of Bible story titles and a chronological index of significant Bible events and stories for quick reference make this a handy kid's tool. Currently out of print but available on CD software.

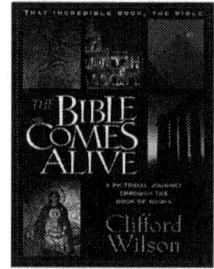

The Bible Comes Alive: Creation to Abraham by Dr. Clifford Wilson ♦ 4-8 9-12

Description: Dr. Wilson, an eminent biblical archaeologist, presents a pictorial summary of his extensive archaeological work in support of his conviction that the Bible is true—historically, scientifically, and theologically. In this volume, Dr.

An Internet-Linked Unit Study

Wilson presents the archaeological and historical evidence supporting the authenticity of the Book of Genesis, and brings to life the age of the patriarchs. Paperback - 176 pages (1997). New Leaf Press; ISBN: 0892213493.

Creation to Christ Timeline Figures (History Through the Ages series) ★ 4-8 9-12

Description: A perfect set of images to use for your Time Line Book! This timeline package covers many people and events of the Bible, Sumer, Babylonian, Mesopotamia, Egypt, Persia, Greece, and the Rise of Rome to the time of Jesus Christ. Included are over 250 detailed figures dating from the beginning of creation to the first century AD, timelines ready to cut and assemble, suggested instructions for use and display, and a handy reference sheet of all the people and events. Each figure is approx. 2.5-3.5" tall. They are printed on a quality cover stock for durability. Cut out images to use in a Time Line Book or place on the wall with provided yellow timeline.

Discover Jesus in Genesis by Larry Edison and Deborah Obeid K-3 4-8

Description: Deborah Obeid and Larry Edison have collaborated together to come up with this book designed to help readers of all ages understand the manner in which Jesus is both the theme and the Promise of Genesis. You'll find many major events from Genesis portrayed in picture form, each displaying the biblical event along with the manner in which God took pains to gradually yet clearly teach His people about the promise and coming of the Messiah. In His actions, God painted a picture so that His people might see Jesus in Genesis. Each chapter consists of one painting on high gloss paper along with a full-page explanation of the biblical text. Be aware there is another book with a very similar title by another author (the other book was a disappointment as it has little to do with the topic). Winepress Publishing (2002). ISBN 157921389832.

Genesis: Finding Our Roots by Ruth Beechick ○― ♦ 4-8 9-12

Description: Provides a unique look at Genesis chapters 1–11, integrating history with art, literature, and other disciplines. It gives startling insights into how ancient art, literature, world history, language, and even ancient myths prove that the Bible is a true historical record. Includes maps, charts, a time line, and beautiful full-color reproductions of ancient art. Hardcover - 112 pages (February 1998). Educational Services Corp.; ISBN: 094031911X. Intended for family study.

God's Story: The Bible Told As One Story by Karyn Henley ♥ K-3

Description: We recommend *The Narrated Bible* and *Nelson's Illustrated Encyclopedia Bible* for older students and this Bible for very young students. Written at a second-grade reading level, this nonfictionalized Bible storybook contains over 800 Bible stories in chronological order. Features include drawings, indexes, and a pictorial time line showing biblical and world events. Omitting genealogies and duplicate passages, Henley presents God's Word as a story that will grab your kids' attention—and keep it! Hardcover - 896 pages (August 1, 1998) Tyndale House Pub.; ISBN: 0842307435. This book was reprinted under the tile *The Day by Day Kid's Bible*.

Recommended in: ♦ several lessons in a unit; ★ several units in a volume; ♥ several volumes. ○― Key Resource for this unit.

Adam to Abraham

The Holman Bible Atlas ♥ 4-8 9-12
Description: Explore the world of the Bible through this visual feast in chronological order. This atlas features hundreds of color photos and maps that show you the land, sites, and archaeology of the entire biblical world. You'll learn about every time period from the Patriarchs to A.D. 300, and every international power from Egypt to Rome. Features 140 full-color photographs, 140 maps, and an index of important biblical places. Hardcover - 256 pages (January 1999). Broadman & Holman Publishers; ISBN: 1558197095. Suitable for older children. For family read-aloud see *Nelson's Illustrated Bible Encyclopedia* below.

The Narrated Bible ♥ 4-8 9-12
Description: *The Narrated Bible* is arranged chronologically, so the readings correspond with the lessons in this book. (Standard Bible references are also given in each lesson if you choose to use another Bible.) Throughout the lessons you will see a Bible icon with numbers. These numbers correspond to page numbers in *The Narrated Bible*. The modern English used is familiar and easy to understand. It is amazingly easy to read through several books of the Bible in one sitting with the story book format. Since it is written in everyday English, the text can be used for dictation and copying lessons (teaching handwriting, grammar, capitalization, and punctuation). The layout of the book is ideal for teaching students how to outline. Hardcover, 1727 pages, Harvest House Publishers, Inc. (1999) ISBN: 0736902392.

74–96
The Narrated Bible

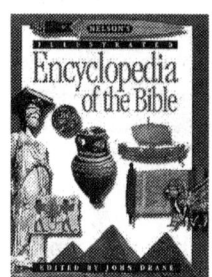

Nelson's Illustrated Bible Encyclopedia ♥ 4-8 9-12
Description: This is an excellent book to use with the Ancient History units. It is an overview of the culture and geography of the Hebrews and their neighbors. Includes lavish illustrations, and hundreds of color photographs, maps, and charts. Drawing on the latest scholarship in archaeology and theology, you get close-up views of the ancient civilizations where people lived under the perceived protection or punishment of their gods, and where the mundane and miraculous overlap. I've gone through dozens and dozens of

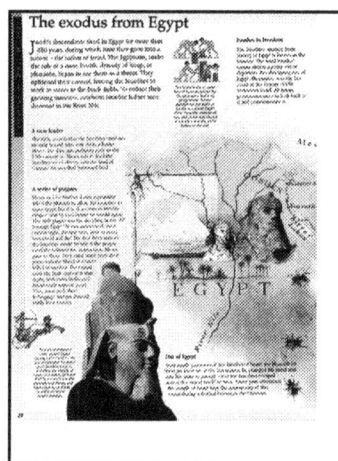
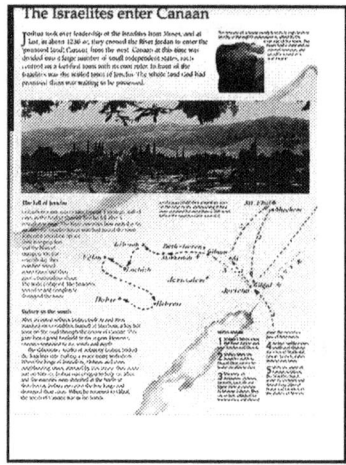

Click on book for purchasing information.

books on this topic and this is my new favorite. An all-in-one, easy-to-understand, heavily illustrated, must-have book to understand Bible times. This is a book you'll use over and over again. There are seven divisions: 1. Outline of Biblical History, 2. People and Empires, 3. The World of the Bible, 4. Religion and Worship, 5. The Life and Teaching of Jesus, 6. The Bible Book by Book, 7. Rapid Factfinder. If you enjoy the visual Eyewitenss books you'll love this book. Paperback: 320 pages, Nelson Reference (2001), ISBN: 0785246142.

Old Testament Bible History by Alfred Edersheim 9-12
Description: Get an unparalleled look at the "big picture" of God's story in the Old Testament. Complete and unabridged, Edersheim's 1890 classic draws on criticism, biblical geography, and archaeology to examine the time from creation to the captivity of Israel and Judah. Alfred Edersheim (1825-89) was a Vienna-born biblical scholar who converted from Judaism to Christianity. A veteran minister and missionary to the Jews of Romania, Edersheim left an enduring and priceless legacy to followers of Christ. Among his most widely read works are *The Life and Times of Jesus the Messiah, The Temple: Its Ministry and Services,* and *Bible History Old Testament.* Hardcover - 1040 pages (1994). Hendrickson; ISBN: 156563165X.

Our Father Abraham: Jewish Roots of the Christian Faith by Marvin Wilson ● 9-12
Description: Recommended in more than eight *Heart of Wisdom Unit Studies.* Wilson explains "Other ancient civilizations produced histories intended primarily to glorify a ruler among his subjects or to exalt that nation in the eyes of the world. Hebrew history, however, was written to glorify the Lord of the universe. It was written to inspire faith and trust in the living God." *Christian Century* magazine listed *Our Father Abraham* as an "all-time bestseller" in its field. Many Christians are regrettably uninformed about the rich Hebrew heritage of the Church. Must-reading for every Christian wanting to delve deeply into the very foundations of the Christian faith. Paperback - 374 pages (1989). W.B. Eerdman's Pub. Co.; ISBN: 0802804233.

Reproducible Maps, Charts, Time Lines and Illustrations: What the Bible Is All About Resources ● 4-8 9-12
Description: Here's a treasure-trove of eye-catching charts, maps, and illustrations to make your lessons come alive—and they're reproducible, so you can use them again and again! Copy and share biblical time lines, an inside view of Solomon's Temple, or a map of Rome. Each "teaching picture" reinforces facts, places, events, and people in God's Word. This is a reference book you will use again and again. Paperback - 287 Pages (January 1998). Gospel Light Publications; ISBN: 0830719385.

Recommended in: ♦ several lessons in a unit; ★ several units in a volume; ● several volumes. ⊙— Key Resource for this unit.

Adam to Abraham

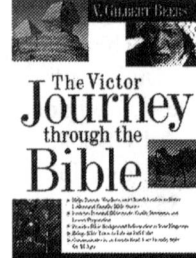

The Victor Journey Through the Bible ♥ 4-8 9-12
Description: This easy-to-read, visual exploration of the Bible allows you to follow the action from Genesis to Revelation. The stories of Scripture will come alive as you travel story-by-story through Bible lands and times. You will discover how ancient people really lived—the foods they ate, the homes they lived in, the clothes they wore, the work they performed. Every library—home, church, and school—will want this complete reference work on its shelves. It will enrich Sunday School lesson preparation, Bible storytelling, family devotions, and Bible study. *The Victor Journey through the Bible* is unparalleled as a user-friendly resource! Includes over 400 colorful pages of photographs, drawings, maps, and charts, more than 100 drawings from objects or monuments of Bible times, over 200 photographs of Bible lands today, photographs of more than 50 archaeological discoveries, scores of reconstructions and diagrams, and dozens of colorful maps. Hardcover: 416 pages, Chariot Victor Books; Reprint edition (1996)ISBN: 156476480X.

Walk Genesis by Jeffrey Enoch Feinberg ♦ 9-12
Description: *Walk Genesis* is a Messianic Jewish devotional commentary that allows you to *Walk Genesis* in your spiritual journey through Eden and the Flood, into the Promised Land, and down into Egypt. This devotional not only focuses on days gone by, but continues into today for all those who desire to walk with God. This commentary follows the weekly Torah (Pentateuch) readings from the synagogue, along with the related Haftarah (Prophets and Writings) readings. Paperback - 238 pages (1999). Lederer Messianic Ministries; ISBN: 1880226758.

Writers INC ♥ ⚬— 9-12
Description: Your student will be referring to this book (or a similar book on your child's level) in many lessons. We do not refer to page numbers in this book because it is frequently revised. Writing, reading, and additional study skills are combined in this comprehensive writing manual. The fundamental principles of writing are explained throughout for quick reference. The process of organizing, researching, and writing a paper is laid out in easy-to-understand language. The book outlines strategies for writing with computers, including instruction in writing multimedia reports and publishing online. Also included is information on thinking and learning skills, such as reviewing, note-taking, test-taking skills, and more. Paperback (August 1995). Write Source; ISBN: 0669388130. Grade level: 9–12, but can be used for grades 4–12 with parents' guidance. See our site for book in this series for younger grades. http://home-schoolunitstudies.com/Resources/writing.htm

Who's Who in the Bible by Stephen Motyer, Peter Dennis (Illustrator) ♥ K-3 4-8
Description: This exceptionally well-illustrated book, like all the best reference books, possesses that hypnotic quality that can lead to hours of random browsing. A good book if you have it on hand but *Nelson's Illustrated Encyclopedia Bible* is much better. Published by the same company which publishes the Eyewitness books, so it has the same look. Hardcover - 64 pages (August 1998). DK Publishing; ISBN: 0789428377.

Adam to Abraham: An Internet-Linked Unit Study

Introduction H10101

Step 1: Excite

The first chapters of Genesis tell the stories of the most dramatic events in the history of mankind. In 11:27 the story changes focus to Abraham and his family. How much do you know about the people who lived between Adam and Abraham? You may have heard the stories of Creation, the Tower of Babel, Abraham, and Noah many times, but do you know the order of the events?

Create a time line using index cards or sticky notes without looking at any references. Using the list below, put each major event and each key person from Genesis on a separate index card. Shuffle the cards and try to line them up in chronological order.

Abel	Enoch	Methuselah
Abraham	The Fall	Noah
Adam	The Flood	Seth
Cain	Ham	Shem
Creation	Japheth	Tower of Babel

Step 2: Examine

To gain an understanding of the Bible, you must first learn some basics. The Bible is made of sixty-six books. written by forty different authors over a period of about 2,000 years. God inspired the writing of these books. There are thirty-nine books in the Old Testament and twenty-seven books in the New Testament.

The Old Testament is divided into three kinds of books:
1. History (first seventeen)
2. Poetry (next five)
3. Prophecy (next seventeen)

The New Testament is divided into three kinds of books:
1. History (four gospels and Acts)
2. Paul's Letters (to churches, to individuals)
3. General

The history books in the Old Testament tell the story of God's people, the Hebrews. There are nine major time frames. Below is an explanation of how we will study each period.

1. Creation . . . .*Creation Unit Study*
2. Patriarchs . . . .*Adam to Abraham Unit Study*
3. Exodus . . . .*Egypt Unit Study*
4. Conquest . . . .*Israel Unit Study*
5. Judges . . . .*Israel Unit Study*
6. Kingdom . . . .*Israel Unit Study*
7. Exile . . . .*Israel Unit Study*

Recommended in: ♦ several lessons in a unit; ★ several units in a volume; ● several volumes. ⌐ Key Resource for this unit.

Adam to Abraham

    8. Return . . . .*Israel Unit Study*
    9. Silence . . . .*Israel Unit Study*

The focus of this Unit Study is on Genesis 1–12, with a brief introduction to the call of Abram and the Land of Canaan. The culture and geography of the Mesopotamian world of the Bible are covered in the *Mesopotamia* Unit Study. The New Testament is studied in the Heart of Wisdom's *Messiah* and *Early Church Unit Studies*.

The first five books of the Bible are called *Torah* (the Law) or the Pentateuch. The first book of the Bible is Genesis. The Book of Genesis is the book of origins. The word *genesis* (Hebrew *b'resheet*) comes from a Greek word that means *origin*, *source*, or *beginning*. The first eleven chapters describe Creation, the Fall, the Flood, and the origin of nations. Chapters 12–50 comprise the ancestral story.

To get an overview of this period, skim through the first eleven chapters of Genesis in a standard Bible or a Bible story book, or watch a video (see resources below) with your family. How well do your cards from Step 1 line up with the actual stories?

Resources

Read or skim any of the resources listed below to get a good overview of the order of the Bible events in Genesis.

K-3	4-8	9-12
The Bible Skim Genesis Chapters 1-11. If you are using the *Narrated Bible* ♥ Skim pages 1-22.	The Bible Skim Genesis Chapters 1-11. If you are using the *Narrated Bible* ♥ Skim pages 1-22.	The Bible Genesis Chapters 1-11. If you are using the *Narrated Bible* ♥ Read pages 1-22.
Discovering Jesus in Genesis ♦ Introduction (iii).	*Discovering Jesus in Genesis* ♦ Introduction (iii).	*Discovering Jesus in Genesis* ♦ Introduction (iii).
Amazing Expedition Bible ♥ Preface (ix-xi).	*Amazing Expedition Bible* ♥ Preface (ix-xi).	*The Bible Comes Alive: Volume One, Creation to Abraham* ★ Section I "Early Genesis Is Factual History."
Who's Who in the Bible ♥ "First People of Genesis" (6-7), "Abraham and His People" (8-9).	*Nelson's Illustrated Encyclopedia of the Bible* ♥ ⚷ "Introduction (9-16) "Understanding the Bible" (194-197)	*Nelson's Illustrated Encyclopedia of the Bible* ♥ ⚷ "Introduction" (9-16) "Understanding the Bible" (194-197)
	The Holman Bible Atlas ♥ "Introduction" (2).	*The Holman Bible Atlas* ♥ "Introduction" (2).
	Who's Who in the Bible ♥ "First People of Genesis" (6-7), "Abraham and His People" (8-9).	*An Historical Survey of the Old Testament* ★ "In the Beginning" (45-72).

An Internet-Linked Unit Study

Audio

What in the World is Going On Here? A Judeo Christian Primer of World History by Diana Waring
Description: These tapes will give you an excellent chronological foundation of God's unfolding plan through history that you can build upon throughout the units. Listen to and discuss the tapes "Creation to the Destruction of Assyria." Order at:
http://www.dianawaring.com/catalog/history-tapes.html#witw1

Video

Genesis (The Bible Collection Series)
Description: The story begins with the creation of man, Adam and Eve's sin, and their temptation by the serpent that led to their banishment from Paradise. The story continues with the first crime committed by mankind (Cain's murder of his brother, Abel,)the condemnation of God, mankind's corruption and evil, and God's regret for having created earth. The choice of Noah, a just and upright man, to build the Ark; the Flood; the eternal Covenant between God and all mankind; all are told through the clear and simple words of an old nomad shepherd. Ninety-three minutes, color. Chordant Distribution Group (1994). ASIN: 8474024579.

In the Beginning
Description: Epic in scope, astounding in detail, and spectacular in special effects, this unforgettable, internationally acclaimed film sweeps you through the first twenty-two chapters of Genesis. You'll witness the majesty of Creation, Noah's faithful obedience, and the destruction of the Tower of Babel. Starring George C. Scott as Abraham and Peter O'Toole as the haunting Angel of God. Two hours, fifty-one minutes,color.. ASIN: 079391020X.

Internet Sources

Genesis Bible Study
Description: Menu page for a series of Bible studies on Genesis 1–11, including introductory articles on how to study and read Genesis narratives. From the Christian Resource Institute.
http://www.cresourcei.org/biblestudy/bbgen1.html

Genesis 1–11: Authentic History?
Description: Discussion about the biblical evidence for Genesis 1–11 to be interpreted as a literal account of history. From ChristianAnswers.Net.
http://www.christiananswers.net/q-aig/aig-c024.html

A Quick Glance at Genesis
Description: The stories of the Bible arranged chronologically, Bible studies, and beginning answers to your Bible questions.
http://www.sbl.org/biblestudies/biblejourney/genesis/issue2.shtm

---

Recommended in: ♦ several lessons in a unit; ★ several units in a volume; ● several volumes. ☻ Key Resource for this unit.

Adam to Abraham

Reading the Old Testament: Genesis 1–11
Description: An outline explaining how Genesis 1–11 conveys basic features of the Hebrew view of God, the universe, and humanity.
http://www.hope.edu/academic/religion/bandstra/RTOT/CH1/CH1_TC.HTM

Word Wise Genesis 1–11
Description: Explains how it is common for us to quote passages from the first eleven chapters of Genesis in a way that is inconsistent with, or contradictory to, the original intention of a passage. http://www.gen2rev.com/wordwise/wwgen1_11a.htm

Step 3: Expand

Choose and complete one of the following activities:

Activity 1: Create an Outline
Create an outline of Genesis chapters 1–12. Refer to the Outline Example.
http://homeschoolunitstudies.com/Bible/Worksheets/outline.htm

Activity 2: Write Summaries
Write a summary paragraph for each of the key events in Genesis chapters 1–12. Refer to Summary Writing. http://homeschoolunitstudies.com/writing.htm#summary
Younger children may narrate or dictate.
1. The creation of the world and Man (chapters 1–2)
2. The corruption of Man, the Fall (chapters 3–5)
3. The destruction of Man, the Flood (chapters 6–9)
4. The dispersion of Man, the nations (chapters 10–11)
5. The calling of Abram (12:1–9) and first entry into Canaan (12:5–7).

Activity 3: Create a Time line or Story Board
Use a sheet of unlined paper and colored markers or pencils. Draw a line with branches showing the Bible events in order: Creation, Adam and Eve, Cain and Abel, corruption, Noah, the Flood, Babel, dispersion, Abram, Canaan, etc. Branch lines from these will hold subtopics. Use different colors for each cluster of information. Ask yourself *who, what, where, when,* and *how*. Here is a smaple to get you started.

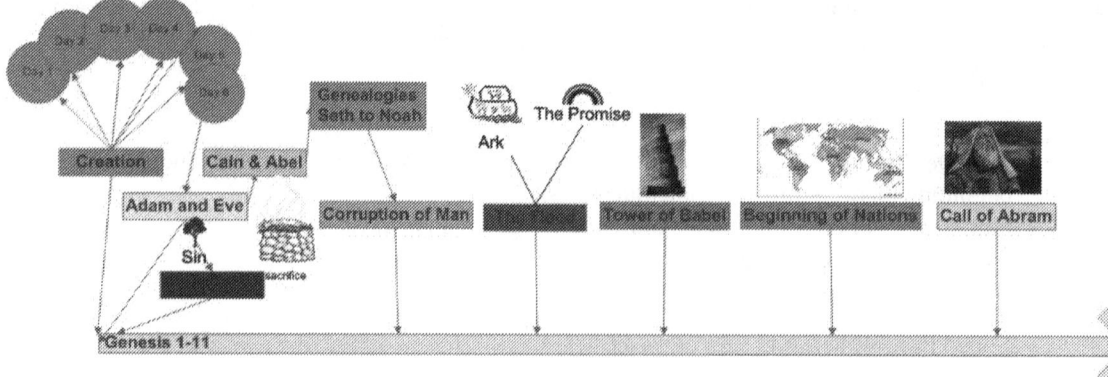

An Internet-Linked Unit Study

Step 4: Excel

Now that you have studied the Book of Genesis you should be able to line up the index cards you created in Step 1 in chronological order. Place the appropriate Bible reference on each card. Use these cards as an outline to begin the first pages in your Time Line Book. Refer to Time Line Book instructions online at http://heartofwisdom.com/Acrobat/timelinebook.PDF.

You may want to make paper people for your Time Line Book. You can dress them with hair and clothes from Bible times. See the back of this book for patterns and ideas. Also see http://heartofwisdom.com/paperpeople.htm.

Heart of Wisdom Paper People

- ❏ Correct all written work to demonstrate correct punctuation and spelling.
- ❏ Correct all written work to demonstrate correct and effective use of grammar.
- ❏ Add to your Writing Notebook the rules for all punctuation and grammar errors you corrected.
- ❏ Record any misspelled words in your Spelling Notebook.
- ❏ Add to your Vocabulary Notebook any new words encountered in this lesson. Include a definition for each word. Use each vocabulary term in a sentence orally or in writing.
- ❏ Add corrected written work or any illustrations to your Portfolio.
- ❏ Add any important people or events to your Time Line Book.

Recommended in: ♦ several lessons in a unit; ★ several units in a volume; ♥ several volumes. ☛ Key Resource for this unit.

Adam to Abraham

Creation H10102

Note: This lesson is merely an overview of Creation. The *Creation* Unit Study examines creation and evolution theories in depth.

The Narrated Bible

Step 1: Excite

Romans chapter 1 tells us that God has planted evidence of Himself throughout His creation so that we are without excuse. The psalmist, in beautiful poetic language, made reference to God's creative work. Here are a few choice allusions: *When I look at thy heavens, the work of thy fingers, the moon and the stars which thou hast established* (Ps. 8:3); *The heavens are telling the glory of God; and the firmament proclaims his handiwork* (Ps. 19:1); *By the word of the Lord the heavens were made, and all their host by the breath of his mouth. He gathered the waters of the sea as in a bottle; he put the deeps in storehouses* (Ps. 33:6,7).

Psalm 136 draws attention to the character of God as displayed in the creation as well as in other mighty works. The worshiper should *give thanks to God, for he is good: his mercy endures forever* (v. 1). In verses 5–8 the psalmist gives details of God's creation, reflecting the Genesis chapter 1 account. The writer of Psalm 148 bids every part of God's creation—the sun, the moon, the shining stars—to praise the name of the Lord, *for he commanded and they were created .(*Ps 148:5) In this way, the psalmist leads us to see the worthiness of God to receive praise and glory for His creation. God tells us about Himself through creation. Our responsibility is to hear His voice and respond to Him.

Watch a video. You may be able to rent these videos from your local Christian bookstore or homeschool support group.

> *God of Creation*
> Description: This video unveils the power and majesty of the world God created—from the smallest organisms to the largest stars in the universe. Order from Moody Video: (800) 842-1223.

> *The Wonders of God's Creation*
> Description: In three spectacular hours, this award-winning series takes you on one of the most exceptional journeys imaginable—from high above planet Earth to the very heart of the human body. Join us and see how the Master Creator reveals Himself through the glorious miracle of Creation! Order from Moody Video: (800) 842-1223.

Step 2: Examine

In the ancient world, Near Eastern creation myths began with either mythological gods (or objects like the sun or moon, treated as gods) in conflict with one another in the heavens. In one story the creator Baal struggles with an adversary, Mot; in another Baal battles the Sea. In the Babylonian creation myth, the god Marduk kills Tiamat (chaos) after a violent battle, which results in creation. The ancient Egyptian myths say that creation began from a chaos of churning, bubbling water, called Nu or Nun, from which Atum (later called Re, Ra, and/or Khepri) created the world. Today's modern evolution myths mirror the ancient myths that somehow our orderly world was created, by accident, out of chaos.

In the Genesis Creation story, God is shown as a personal God in complete control, calling the entire universe into creation by His spoken Word. Human beings, male and female, are created in the image and likeness of God. Genesis emphasizes the awesome power of our Creator, while illustrating that human beings are the clear focus of God's loving concern.

What a difference between the pagan stories and the Genesis story! All the myths are cold, dead, lifeless, uncaring, while the Creation story is warm, loving, and alive. Christians know that our heavenly Father created the world and each person for a reason. *By faith we understand that the universe was formed at God's command.* (Heb. 11:3). Knowing this gives us value, a special sense of comfort and joy, and hope for our lives and our future. Those who believe that life gradually evolved from single cells into complex forms find no real meaning in life, believing that they and everything around them resulted from a freak accident.

Dr. Albert Green, founder of Alta Vista College, stated in his book *Thinking Christianly*[1]:

> A biblical way of looking at creation will have consequences on your life. As the Holy Spirit grips your heart with the realization that creation reveals God and can be offered back to Him in our ordinary daily activities, praise will well up in your heart as never before. Further, you will find your life come together with new integrity. No more sacred/secular dualism! Christ really is Lord of all! What a glorious message the Gospel is!

> Think of a lovely rosebud in a vase. Where is the beauty of the flower? Is it in the bud itself? A botanist will tell us the flower is simply a bunch of atoms and molecules batting around in empty space. Is the beauty in the retina of our eyes, or in our brains? No, it is God's beauty, reflected back to us from the petals of the rosebud.

> God makes all pleasures. The devil misuses them; he does not make them. If we learn to recognize every pleasure as a shaft of God's glory touching our hearts, that recognition will become an unspoken prayer of praise and worship. Probably that is what Paul means by admonishing us to pray without ceasing.

Jesus was there with God in the beginning of time: *He is before all things, and in Him all things hold together* (Col. 1:17). When replying to a question from theologians, *Jesus said unto them, Verily, verily, I say unto you, Before Abraham was, I am* (John 8:58). In a prayer Jesus said, "*Father, I will that they also, whom thou hast given me, be with me where I am; that they may behold my glory, which thou hast given me: for thou lovedst me before the foundation of the world*" (John 17:24).

Required Reading
You've probably heard the Creation story. This time, as you read or listen, take time to reflect on how the Creation story refveals the person of God. Observe the distinct sequences, order, consistency, and priorities. Most English versions of the Bible translate *Elohim* as "GOD" (all caps) and *YHVH (Yahweh)* as "LORD" (all caps). *YHVH* is used when the Bible stresses God's personal relationship with his people. *Elohim* refers to God as the Creator of the whole universe and the source of all life. For this reading, replace the titles for GOD or LORD with Elohim and Yahweh. Notice from your reading that evening always precedes morning: *And the evening and the morning were the first day* (Gen. 1:5). And the

Adam to Abraham

evening and the morning were the second day (Gen 1:8). Even today, the Jewish people consider the beginning of a day to be at sunset the evening before. Monday actually begins at Sunday sundown. The Sabbath begins Friday at sundown.

Suggested Resources

If you would like to know more about Creation, explore any of the resources listed below.

K-3	4-8	9-12
The Bible. Genesis read aloud the Creation story in Genesis chapters 1–2 with your family. If you are using the *Narrated Bible* ♥ Read pages 1-3.		
Read John 1:1–18, Eph. 1:3–14, Col. 1:15–20, and Heb. 1:1–4 for further insight on God's eternal nature.		
Discovering Jesus in Genesis ♦ "Creation: The Beginning" (4-5).	*Discovering Jesus in Genesis* ♦ "Creation: The Beginning" (4-5).	*Discovering Jesus in Genesis* ♦ "Creation: The Beginning" (4-5).
Amazing Expedition Bible ♥ "In the Beginning" (20-21).	*Amazing Expedition Bible* ♥ When Time Began (3-4).	*The Bible Comes Alive: Volume One, Creation to Abraham* ★ Section II "In the Beginning."
God's Story ♥ "When Time Began" (3-4)	*Adam and His Kin* Chapter 1 "The Beginning of Time" and Chapter 2 "In the Garden."	*Adam and His Kin* Chapter 1 "The Beginning of Time" and Chapter 2 "In the Garden."
	The Victor Journey Through the Bible ♥ "Creation" (10-11).	*The Victor Journey Through the Bible* ♥ "Creation" (10-11).
	Genesis: Finding Our Roots ⚷ Unit 1 "God's Book of Creation."	*Genesis: Finding Our Roots* ⚷ Unit 1 "God's Book of Creation."
		A Historical Survey of the Old Testament ★ "In the Beginning: The Ancient Near East World" (45-48).
		Bible History: Old Testament ★ Chapter 1 of Volume 1. It discusses the importance of Jesus Christ in Creation.

An Internet-Linked Unit Study

Internet Sources

Creation - Man in the Garden of Eden - The Fall
Description: Discusses the importance of Jesus Christ in Creation from chapter 1, volume 1 of *Bible History: Old Testament*, by Alfred Edersheim.
http://philologos.org/__eb-bhot/vol_I/ch01.htm

God's Creation
Description: Part 1 of "God's Story: From Creation to Eternity" from ChristianAnswers.net. (Follow the "next" buttons on the bottom of each page.)
http://www.christiananswers.net/godstory/creation1.html

The Literal Week of Creation
Description: Article by Henry Morris from the Institute for Creation Research.
http://www.icr.org/pubs/btg-a/btg-113a.htm

The 6 Days of Creation
Description: An excellent study, the first part of *Old Testament Bible Study: Creation to Abraham, Genesis 1 to Genesis 12*. Includes the three basic views concerning the origin of the universe. http://www.bibletruths.net/Archives/BTAR114.htm

Step 3: Expand

Choose and complete one of the following activities:

Activity 1: Write a Poem
Write a poem about creation. Refer to "Writing Poetry" in *Writers Inc*, and to Ps. 148:1–6 and Isa. 45:18.

Activity 2: Learn Hebrew Words
Look up each of these words in a Hebrew lexicon. Add the word, its phonetic spelling, and its meaning to your Hebrew Notebook. See *The Old Testament Hebrew Lexicon:* http://bible.crosswalk.com/Lexicons/OldTestamentHebrew/

The Hebrew word for *created* is *bara*; Hebrew actually has several words for *creating, making, building,* or *forming,* or *created—bara* is used only in referring to God in the Hebrew Bible. It occurs in Gen. 1:1, also in vv.21,27. Usually, *bara* is understood to be creation *ex nihilo,* "out of nothing." Only God can call things into existence that do not exist.
The Hebrew word *rosh* means "head." It is used in the word *Rosh HaShanah* (New Year or head of the year), *rosh avot* (head of the family), *rosh pinah* (cornerstone of head of the stone), and *Rosh Chodesh* (head of the month or new moon).
Genesis chapter 1 contains the phrase "The heavens and the earth." The Hebrew word for *heavens* is *et ha-shamayim;* it is plural, and is equivalent to the New Testament term *heavenly places,* or *the heavenlies.* The Hebrew word for *earth* is *eh'-rets*. It implies the whole earth (as opposed to a part).

Recommended in: ♦ several lessons in a unit; ★ several units in a volume; ♥ several volumes. ☞ Key Resource for this unit.

Heart of Wisdom Publishing

Adam to Abraham

Activity 3: Make a Creation Display
Create a miniature quilt wall hanging. Print out the images below from our web site. Trace designs on the paper side of a paper-backed fusible webbing such as Aleen's Hot-Stitch® or Wonder Under®. Following the manufacturer's directions, fuse to the wrong side of your chosen fabrics. Trim shapes on the line (except for edges which will lie underneath another shape). Cut all areas as smoothly as possible. Lay all pieces in place and fuse to the background fabric at one time. If desired, use decorative machine stitching or fabric paint to secure all raw edges. (Joining the squares and quilting directions are on our web site). Alternative #1: Make a paper quilt. Create six blocks on a sheet of construction paper. Using a pencil, make an outline of symbols on a sheet of construction paper. Cut out shapes of different colors of construction paper and glue them to the paper, applying the shapes to the main sheet. Alternative #2: Print out images in black ink and color with markers or crayons. Alternative #3: Print out images in color and add to your Portfolio Notebook.
http://heartofwisdom.com/worksheets/creationdays.htm

Images available for printing from http://heartofwisdom.com/worksheets/creationdays.htm

Activity 4: Study Art

Renaissance artist Michelangelo devised an elaborate scheme for the decoration of the Sistine Chapel ceiling, which he painted between 1508 and 1512. It features nine scenes from the Book of Genesis, including the *Creation of Adam*, the *Creation of Eve*, the *Temptation and Fall of Adam and Eve*, and the *Flood*. These centrally located narratives are surrounded by images of prophets and sibyls on marble thrones, and by other biblical subjects. Find and study, at a library, a museum or on the Internet, any of these paintings by Michelangelo (*be aware this artwork contains nudity* select another activity if you find this one offensive.). Write a description of the paintings in the Sistine Chapel.
http://christianity.about.com/library/weekly/blsistineceilingcreation.htm

Activity 5: Copy Passages

Copy by hand or typing, two or more paragraphs from your research, or have someone dictate the passage(s) to you. Younger students may copy one or two sentences or narrate (tell back) what has been learned.

Activity 6: Complete Worksheets

Print out and complete the *The Creative Days* worksheets and puzzles.
http://www.calvarychapel.org/children/site/pdf/Old/Curr001.pdf

Activity 7: Go on a Nature Walk

Go on a walk and observe the beauty of God's creation. Think about your favorite things. When you return from your walk, work together to construct a poem describing the things you thought of as beautiful. Read Ps. 148:1–6 for inspiration.

Step 4: Excel

- ☐ Correct all written work to demonstrate correct punctuation and spelling.
- ☐ Correct all written work to demonstrate correct and effective use of grammar.
- ☐ Add to your Writing Notebook the rules for all punctuation and grammar errors you corrected.
- ☐ Record any misspelled words in your Spelling Notebook.
- ☐ Add to your Vocabulary Notebook any new words encountered in this lesson. Include a definition for each word. Use each vocabulary term in a sentence orally or in writing.
- ☐ Add corrected written work or any illustrations to your Portfolio.
- ☐ Add any important people or events to your Time Line Book.
- ☐ Share with a friend or family member an activity you completed for this lesson. Explain to them what you have learned.

Footnote
1. Green, Albert. 1990. *Thinking Christianly*, Seattle, WA: Alta Vista College Press.
2. Lindsay, Dennis. G. 1999, c1995. *The ABC's of Evolutionism: Ape-man, Batman, Catwoman, and Other Evolutionary Fantasies*. Dallas, TX: Christ for the Nations.

Recommended in: ♦ several lessons in a unit; ★ several units in a volume; ● several volumes. ⌐ Key Resource for this unit.

Adam to Abraham

Garden of Eden H10103

Step 1: Excite

The Narrated Bible

The Bible says that when God created a thing, *He saw that it was good.* The Lord God created a perfect environment for Adam and Eve. The Garden was certainly a most wonderful place. Adam sinned, however, and this perfect environment became corrupted. Not much is written about the Garden, so we must picture it using our imagination as a glimpse of what God will do in the future. God, in His timing, will once again make a perfect world. In this future place, we know that *The wolf also shall dwell with the lamb, and the leopard shall lie down with the kid; and the calf and the young lion and the fatling together; and a little child shall lead them. And the cow and the bear shall feed; their young ones shall lie down together: and the lion shall eat straw like the ox. And the sucking child shall play on the hole of the asp* [snake], *and the weaned child shall put his hand on the cockatrice'* [serpent or asp] *den.* (Isa. 11:6–8).

Close your eyes and imagine what it must have been like to be in a glorious garden of incredible beauty and harmony that was free of any trace of sin and its consequences. Imagine daily life walking in perfect harmony with the animals. Imagine how wonderful the food tasted.

The Bible says that mountains, hills, trees, and animals eagerly look for the coming of the Lord (Isa. 55:12–13; Rom. 8:19; Psm. 96:11–13; 98:7–9), for they know that one day the earth will be set free from the curse of sin. The Earth may again experience an environment like the one Adam and Eve knew in the Garden of Eden. The Tree of Life (Gen. 2:9) in the Garden of Eden appears again in Rev. 2:7 and 22:2, when a sinless environment is once again provided for humanity. In Eden's paradise, we see a shadow of the majesty and glory of the heavenly home that awaits us if we have trusted in God's Son.

Step 2: Examine

The Garden of Eden was also called the *Garden of the Lord* (Gen. 13:10; Isa. 51:3) and the *Garden of God* (Ezek. 28:13). Gen. 2:11–14 tell us that four rivers flowed from this garden: the Pison, the Gihon, the Hiddekel, and the Euphrates.

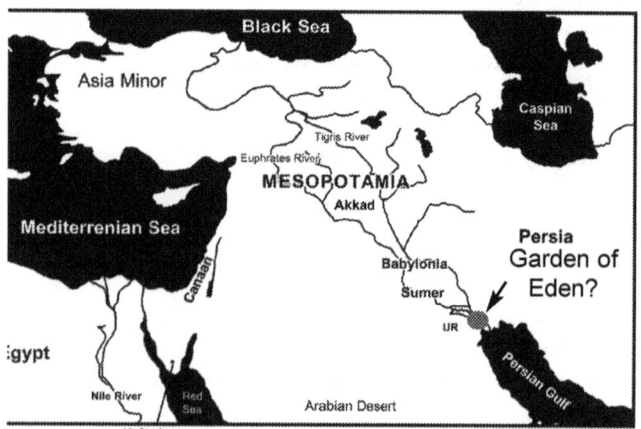

The *Bible Knowledge Commentary* explains:

The garden was probably in the area of the Persian Gulf, judging from the place names in these verses. If the geography of that area was the same after the Flood as before, then the Tigris (lit., Hiddeqel) and the Euphrates, the third and fourth rivers, can be identified. The first of the four rivers, Pishon, was in Havilah, in north-central Arabia, east of Palestine. The second river, Gihon, was in Cush, probably not Ethiopia but possibly the land of the Cassites (kasûsûu in Akk.) in the mountains east of Mesopotamia.

ADAM 36

Wherever the Garden of Eden was located, we know that it was too beautiful to describe. It was a utopia. God commanded the man to take care of the Garden, to "tend and keep it." This task was a gift from God. *I know that nothing is better for them than to rejoice, and to do good in their lives. And also that every man should eat and drink, and enjoy the good of all his labor—it is the gift of God* (Eccl. 3:12,13).

Suggested Resources

Explore any of the resources listed below for more information on the Graden of Eden.

Internet Sources

K-3	4-8	9-12
Read more about the Garden of Eden in Genesis. 2:8–14. If you are using the *Narrated Bible* ♥ Read pages 4.		
Discovering Jesus in Genesis ♦ "Crowned with Glory" (6-7).	*Discovering Jesus in Genesis* ♦ "Crowned with Glory" (6-7).	*Discovering Jesus in Genesis* ♦ "Crowned with Glory" (6-7).
God's Story ♥ "Adam's Helper" (4-5)	*Adam and His Kin* ♦ Chapter 2 "In the Garden"	*Adam and His Kin* ♦ Chapter 2 "In the Garden"
Amazing Expedition Bible ♥ "The Story of Creation" (21).	*Genesis: Finding Our Roots* ♦ Unit 2 "Book of Adam."	*Genesis: Finding Our Roots* ♦ Unit 2 "Book of Adam."
	The Holman Bible Atlas ♥ "The Garden of Eden" (33).	*The Holman Bible Atlas* ♥ "The Garden of Eden" (33).
	Bible History: Old Testament ★ Chapter 1 "Creation - Man in the Garden of Eden."	*Bible History: Old Testament* ★ Chapter 1 "Creation - Man in the Garden of Eden."

ⓘ *Creation - Man in the Garden of Eden*
Description: Chapter 1 from *Bible History: Old Testament*, by Alfred Edersheim.
http://philologos.org/__eb-bhot/vol_I/ch01.htm

ⓘ *The Garden of Eden*
Description: Article from *The Condensed Biblical Cyclopedia*.
http://bible.crosswalk.com/Encyclopedias/CondensedBiblicalCyclopedia/cbe.cgi?number=T3

ⓘ *Garden of Eden Jigsaw Puzzle*
Description: Online puzzle that lets you choose your level: easy (eight pieces) to difficult (eighty pieces). http://www.dltk-bible.com/genesis/chapter2-puzzle.htm

ⓘ *In Search of Eden*
Description: The Discovery Channel puts a scientific spin on the story of Adam and Eve. Site includes several paintings of the Garden by artists of varying faiths and cultures

---

Recommended in: ♦ several lessons in a unit; ★ several units in a volume; ♥ several volumes. ☛ Key Resource for this unit.

Adam to Abraham

(caution: contains nudity). Includes a very interesting interactive map that lets you click on each river and on other areas for details. Order online at
http://tlc.discovery.com/convergence/eden/eden.html

Where Was the Garden of Eden?
Description: Bible study from "Daily Bible Study."
http://www.execulink.com/%7Ewblank/20000110.htm

Step 3: Expand

Choose and complete one of the following activities:

Activity 1: Copy Passages
Copy (by hand or typing) two or more Bible references about the Garden of Eden: Gen. 2:8–17; 3:23,24; 4:16; Isa. 51:3; Ezekiel 28:13; 31:9,16,18; 36:35; and Joel 2:3.

Activity 2: Draw and Narrate
Draw a picture of what you think the Garden of Eden was like. Students should narrate or tell the story of the garden of Eden. Include several details.

Activity 3: Complete Worksheets
Print out and complete the online worksheets and puzzles at
http://www.calvarychapel.org/children/site/pdf/Old/Curr003.pdf

Activity 4: Write an Essay
Write an essay about what you imagine the Garden to have been like. The essay should be at least 100 words, but not more than 500 words. Refer to "Structure of the Traditional Essay" and "Sample of a Traditional Essay" in *Writers Inc,* or "How to Write an Essay" at http://homeschoolunitstudies.com/writing.htm#essays

Step 4: Excel

- ❏ Correct all written work to demonstrate correct punctuation and spelling.
- ❏ Correct all written work to demonstrate correct and effective use of grammar.
- ❏ Copy any all grammar or punctuation rules you corrected into your Writing Notebook.
- ❏ Record any misspelled words in your Spelling Notebook.
- ❏ Add any unfamiliar or new words to your Vocabulary Notebook.
- ❏ Add corrected written work or any illustrations to your Portfolio.
- ❏ Share with a friend or family member the activity you completed for this lesson. Explain to them what you have learned.

Adam and Eve H10104

Step 1: Excite

The Narrated Bible

*And the LORD God caused a deep sleep to fall upon Adam, and he slept:
and he took one of his ribs, and closed up the flesh instead thereof;
And the rib, which the LORD God had taken from man, made he a woman,
and brought her unto the man. And Adam said,
This is now bone of my bones, and flesh of my flesh:
she shall be called Woman, because she was taken out of Man.
(Gen. 2:21–23).*

Why didn't God make Eve out of the ground in the same way He created Adam? Some Christians believe that men have one less rib than women do, but this isn't true. It's probable that Adam's rib grew back. Thoracic (chest) surgeons routinely remove ribs from patients' rib cages for grafting bone that will manufacture new bone, because the rib is the ideal bone for regeneration; the rib or part of the rib grows back.

And God said, Let us make man in our image, after our likeness (Gen. 1:26).

Discuss the meanings of the words *image* and *likeness*. God did not make the animals with the same intelligence as that of man, or with man's ability to think, reason, and communicate. Some people have a poor self-image. But God made each person special, with unique gifts and talents.

Make a list of things that you like about yourself (do not include physical appearance). When we realize that there is good inside, then we can find ways to use that good for God. How does it feel to know that God has shared His image with you?

Step 2: Examine

On the sixth day of Creation, God created all the living creatures and, "in his own image," man both "male and female." The Hebrew word for Adam is ~da it means "mankind," "men and women," "people." The woman's name was Eve (Hebrew *hawwah*, similar to *hayyah*, "life"). The Genesis 1 account of man's creation stresses that man was created to have dominion, and secondly, that God gave man the privilege of responsibility.

The first act of Adam was to give names to the beasts of the field and the fowls of the air. After that, God caused a deep sleep to fall upon him, and while he was unconscious, God took one of his ribs, and made a woman. God presented her to Adam. Adam received her as his wife, and said, "This is now bone of my bone, and flesh of my flesh: she shall be called woman, because she was taken out of man." He called her Eve, because she was the mother of all living beings. God then blessed the couple, told them to be "fruitful and multiply," and gave them dominion over all other living things.

Recommended in: ♦ several lessons in a unit; ★ several units in a volume; ● several volumes. ⌕ Key Resource for this unit.

Heart of Wisdom Publishing

If God had formed Eve from the ground, Adam might have felt differently toward her. But Eve shared both Adam's flesh and his spirit. Men and women are formed of one flesh. The woman was taken from his side to remain at his side, to be a "helpmeet." There are two responsibilities for the couple, first, to be fruitful, and second, to subdue the earth.

Adam was the head of the human race. He was created perfect and given dominion over the earth. As the Bible presents Adam as the first man, Christ is referred to as the last Adam (1 Cor. 15:45). Adam was made in the image of God, Christ is the image of the invisible God (Col. 1:15). Jesus Christ is the head of redeemed humanity (Eph 5:23). Since Christ died once for all (Heb. 7:27; 9:28; 10:10–14), there will never be the need for any further *Adam*. Hence He is the last Adam.

> *And so it is written, The first man Adam was made a living soul; the last Adam was made a quickening spirit. Howbeit that was not first which is spiritual, but that which is natural; and afterward that which is spiritual. 47 The first man is of the earth, earthy: the second man is the Lord from heaven.* (1 Cor 15:45-47).

When Jesus was crucified on the cross, He was crucified as the Last Adam:

The first Adam was lord over a limited domain, the last Adam is Lord of all (Acts 10:36).

The first Adam was tempted and failed the test, and in him, we all continue to sin and die. The Last Adam was tempted, as was the first, but remained sinless and lived a perfect life of righteousness and in him, we all can receive eternal life.

The first Adam disobeyed God. The last Adam was *obedient unto death, even the death of the cross.* (Philippians 2:8).

The first Adam began with everything provided for him in the Garden of Eden and he lost everything. The Last Adam began with nothing in a stable and gained everything.

The first Adam gave life to all his descendants. The Last Adam, Jesus Christ, communicates HIs life and light to all men, and gives eternal life to those who receive Him and believe on His name (John 1:1–14).

The Hebrew word for *side* is *tsela*, the Greek word, *pleura*. The same Greek word occurs when Adam's rib was removed from his side and in the crucifixion account, when the soldiers pierced Jesus' side (John 19:34–36).

An Internet-Linked Unit Study

Suggested Resources

If you would like to know more about Adam and Eve, explore any of the resources listed below.

K-3	4-8	9-12
Read about the creation of Adam and Eve Genesis 1:26–31 and Genesis 2:4–7. What was God's attitude about His creation and about Adam in particular? If you are using the *Narrated Bible* ♥ Read the last part of page 2 to the end of page 6.		
God's Story ♥ "Adam's Helper" (4).	*Adam and His Kin* ♦ Chapter 1 "The Beginning of Time."	*Adam and His Kin* ♦ Chapter 1 "The Beginning of Time."
Who's Who in the Bible ♥ "The First People of Genesis" (6-7).	*Who's Who in the Bible* ♥ "The First People of Genesis" (6-7).	*Who's Who in the Bible* ♥ "The First People of Genesis" (6-7).
	Genesis: Finding Our Roots ♦ Unit 2 "Book of Adam."	*Genesis: Finding Our Roots* ♦ Unit 2 "Book of Adam."

TV and Video

ⓘ *Biography: Adam and Eve*
Description: This simple story of temptation and innocence lost has endured and resonated in the hearts of Westerners for thousands of years. This program combines expert interviews, abundant location footage, and rare paintings and artifacts to create a unique portrait of the two people who started it all. This is an in-depth look at Adam and Eve, the man and woman who gave humans their humanity. Watch local listings for A&E viewing time, or order the video (available in some public libraries).
http://store.aetv.com/html/catalog/vp01.jhtml?id=14089&AID=10273739&PID=1132417

Internet Sources

ⓘ *What Was Adam Like?*
Description: Article from *Answers Online, Answers in Genesis Ministries*.
http://www.answersingenesis.org/docs/3783.asp

ⓘ *Adam*
Description: Brief biography of Adam from *BibleTutor.com*.
http://www.lutherproductions.com/bibletutor/demo/level1/program/start/people/adam.htm

ⓘ *The Seed of the Woman*
Description: Bible study explaining the promise of salvation.
http://www.abideinchrist.org/messages/gen3v15.html

Recommended in: ♦ several lessons in a unit; ★ several units in a volume; ♥ several volumes. ⓞ— Key Resource for this unit.

Adam to Abraham

ⓘ *The Last Adam*
Description: Bible study devotional from *Christ in the Old Testament*
http://www.abideinchrist.org/messages/1cor1520.html

ⓘ *Adam & Eve: Excuses, Excuses, Excuses*
Description: Modern-day parable between father and son, relating to Adam and Eve's excuses for sin.
http://conline.net/readings/devotions/901956466678.html

ⓘ *The Creation of Man*
Description: An excellent study, part of *Old Testament Bible Study: Creation to Abraham, Genesis 1 to Genesis 12*.
http://www.bible-truth.org/gen2.htm

ⓘ *Regenerating Ribs*
Description: Interesting article from *Answers in Genesis Ministries*, explaining that thoracic (chest) surgeons routinely remove ribs, which often grow back in whole or in part.
http://www.answersingenesis.org/docs/4145.asp

Step 3: Expand

Choose and complete one of the following activities:

Activity 1: Make a Scrapbook Page
Create a scrapbook page by making a background of a beautiful garden (or purchasing garden or animal border paper at any store that carries scrapbook supplies). Look through coloring books for images. Use Paper People in the back of this book to create Adam and Eve (cover clothing areas with green plants using cut outs, die cuts, or stickers). Get creative, consider a plant border, adding animal stickers, lettering, journaling Bible verses on a section of the page, etc. Send us a photo or scan of your page to share with others. See sample pages at http://HeartofWisdom.com/studentswork.htm

Activity 2: Write a Story
Write the story of the creation of Adam and Eve in your own words (minimum 150 words). Refer to "Writing about an Event" in *Writers Inc*. (Younger students may dictate the story.)

Activity 3: Contrast and Compare
Make a contrast-and-compare graphic of the *First Adam* and the *Last Adam*, Jesus. 1 Cor. 15:45,47 gives two names, or titles, for Jesus: He is spoken of as the Last Adam and as the Second Man. As the Last Adam, Christ is the sum total of humanity; as the Second Man, He is the Head of a new race. So we have here two unions, the one relating to His death and the other to His resurrection. Visit the URL below for instructions.
http://homeschoolunitstudies.com/TG/teacherhelps/contrast.htm

An Internet-Linked Unit Study

Activity 4: Answer Questions
Answer the following:
1. Who named Eve? (Gen. 2:23; 3:20)
2. Who was first fooled by Satan? (Gen. 3; 2 Cor. 11:3; 1 Tim. 2:14)
3. How does the serpent display craftiness in tempting the woman?
4. Compare Genesis chapter 3, verses 4 and 5 to 3:22. Did the serpent lie?
5. What is the woman's punishment given in Gen. 3:16?
6. Who were the children of Adam and Eve? (Gen. 4:1,2,25; 5:3,4)
7. How old was Adam when he died? (Gen. 5:5)
8. Why is Christ referred to as the Last Adam? (1 Cor. 15:45)

Activity 5: Learn Hebrew Words
Look up each of these words in a Hebrew lexicon. Add the word, its phonetic spelling, and its meaning to your Hebrew Notebook. The Hebrew word *adam* is ~da (phonetic - aw-dam'); it means *mankind*, or *people*. The Hebrew word for *eve* is hwwx (phonetic - khav-vaw'); it means *life* or *living*. The Hebrew word for *side* is *tsela* (phonetic - tsay-law'); it means *side*, rib, or *beam*.
http://bible.crosswalk.com/Lexicons/OldTestamentHebrew/

Activity 6: Complete Worksheets
Complete the worksheets and puzzles for *God Makes Adam and Eve*.
http://www.calvarychapel.org/children/site/pdf/Old/Curr002.pdf

Activity 7: Illustrate a Comic
Draw a comic-book page, complete with conversations in "bubbles," depicting the story of Adam and Eve.

Step 4: Excel

☐ Correct all written work to demonstrate correct punctuation and spelling.
☐ Correct all written work to demonstrate correct and effective use of grammar.
☐ Add to your Writing Notebook the rules for all punctuation and grammar errors you corrected.
☐ Record any misspelled words in your Spelling Notebook.
☐ Add to your Vocabulary Notebook any new words encountered in this lesson. Include a definition for each word. Use each vocabulary term in a sentence orally or in writing.
☐ Add corrected written work or any illustrations to your Portfolio.
☐ Add any important people or events to your Time Line Book.
☐ Share with a friend or family member an activity you completed for this lesson. Explain to them what you have learned.

Recommended in: ◆ several lessons in a unit; ★ several units in a volume; ● several volumes. ⊙— Key Resource for this unit.

Heart of Wisdom Publishing

Adam to Abraham

The Fall H10105

Step 1: Excite

The Narrated Bible

There was a fall and rebellion before the creation of Adam. Do you know the story?

Angels existed before Adam was created (Job 38:4-7). Scholars disagree about the timing of the creation of angels but we do know they existed before Adam. Lucifer was an angel of authority. He was honored in heaven as "the anointed cherub that covereth." He was created with freedom of choice but allowed evil to enter into his heart and mind and introduced evil into the world.

Ezek. 28:12-15 describes Lucifer as full of wisdom and perfect in beauty. Eze. 28:15 says, *You were perfect in your ways from the day you were created, till iniquity was found in you.* Pride caused the wisdom he was given to become twisted and corrupted. He incited rebellion among a group of angels that helped him attempt overcome God Almighty. There was war in heaven. God and true, loyal angels prevailed; Lucifer and his sympathizers were expelled from heaven and they are still awaiting their final judgment. Lucifer means *the bright and shining one;* after his fall, however, his name was changed to Satan, which means *adversary*. By trying to rise higher than God, Satan became the enemy of God and the enemy of God's people.

Satan tempts Eve by twisting and rationalizing the command of God. Make a list of at least ten sins committed today that man tries to rationalize. Look over your list and discuss the motivations for the listed sins.

Step 2: Examine

God created the perfect environment in the Garden of Eden. Then He created Adam. Adam was God's masterpiece, created in God's own image. From Adam, all mankind descended. Adam had the first personal relationship with God—he walked with God, talked with God, and he tended God's creation. When Adam and Eve were placed in the beautiful garden they had everything they could desire including an awesome relationship with their Creator! But Satan was also there.

Satan assumed the form of a serpent and enters Eden to tempt Eve. He twisted God's commands and convinces Eve God's law is too strict. He distorts Eve's view of God by causing her to question God's motives. Satan finally convinced Eve that God is selfishness and only forbade the fruit to keep her from being like God.

Matthew Henry explains,

> He denies that there was any danger in it, insisting that, though it might be the transgressing of a precept, yet it would not be the incurring of a penalty. These were the baits with which he covered his hook.

ADAM 44

1. "Your eyes shall be opened; you shall have much more of the power and pleasure of contemplation than now you have; you shall fetch a larger compass in your intellectual views, and see further into things than now you do." He speaks as if now they were but dim-sighted, and short-sighted, in comparison of what they would be then.

2. "You shall be as gods, as Elohim, mighty gods; not only omniscient, but omnipotent too;" or, "You shall be as God himself, equal to him, rivals with him; you shall be sovereigns and no longer subjects, self-sufficient and no longer dependent." A most absurd suggestion! As if it were possible for creatures of yesterday to be like their Creator that was from eternity.

3. "You shall know good and evil, that is, every thing that is desirable to be known." To support this part of the temptation, he abuses the name given to this tree: it was intended to teach the practical knowledge of good and evil, that is, of duty and disobedience; and it would prove the experimental knowledge of good and evil, that is, of happiness and misery. In these senses, the name of the tree was a warning to them not to eat of it; but he perverts the sense of it, and gives it to their destruction, as if this tree would give them a speculative notional knowledge of the natures, kinds, and originals, of good and evil. And,

4. All this presently: "In the day you eat thereof you will find a sudden and immediate change for the better." Now in all these insinuations he aims to beget in them, First, Discontent with their present state, as if it were not so good as it might be, and should be. Note, No condition will of itself bring contentment, unless the mind be brought to it. Adam was not easy, no, not in paradise, nor the angels in their first state, Jude 6. Secondly, Ambition of preferment, as if they were fit to be gods. Satan had ruined himself by desiring to be like the Most High (Isa. 14:14), and therefore seeks to infect our first parents with the same desire, that he might ruin them too.[1]

Satan is a subtle liar from the beginning (John 8:44), all his lies have a common theme: one can sin and get away with it. But death is the penalty for sin (Gen. 2:17). The beautiful harmony of God's creation was shattered by the entry of human sin.

When a man obeys God, he demonstrates his complete faith in the wisdom of God. Beginning with Adam, God has consistently demonstrated His will in the context of instructions or commands. Breaking the commands is disobedience and causes separation from God. God's commands are never unfair or too strict but man, being a sinner by nature, falls short in obeying God.

Lured by the temptation of instant pleasure Eve succumbed and persuaded her husband also to eat. Their opened eyes saw only their naked bodies, and they attempted to hide from each other and from God. Sin unchecked produces more evil. When the heart of a person no longer looks toward God, every thought and every action becomes based on sin. It is this condition in which man found himself, and it is this condition that God was sad to see. Since Adam, sin has kept man separated from God.

Recommended in: ♦ several lessons in a unit; ★ several units in a volume; ● several volumes. ☞ Key Resource for this unit.

Adam to Abraham

After the Fall, God shows His love and mercy by providing a sacrifice for the sin. God took a sacrificial animal (probably a lamb because Abel is revealed as a shepherd in the next chapter), slew it before the eyes of Adam and Eve and wrapped the skins about their naked bodies. The animal would be an innocent substitute.

For years, God's people used animals as an annual reminder of their sins. But the blood of animals cannot really remove the guilt of sin. God provided the ultimate sacrifice later when He sent His son, without sin, to die for the sins of all mankind. Jesus was the final and full sacrifice for sin forever (Heb. 9:28; Romans 5:8). As believers in Christ, we are clothed with His perfect righteousness.

Suggested Resources

If you would like to know more about the Fall of Man, explore any of the resources listed below.

K-3	4-8	9-12
Read about the Fall of Adam and Eve in Genesis 3:1-24. Then read Romans. 5:12,15,19. If you are using the *Narrated Bible* ♥ Read pages 5 and 6 and the last half of age 1567.		
Discovering Jesus in Genesis ♦ "The Promised Battle"(8-9) "Out of the Garden" (10-11).	*Discovering Jesus in Genesis* ♦ "The Promised Battle"(8-9) "Out of the Garden" (10-11).	*Discovering Jesus in Genesis* ♦ "The Promised Battle"(8-9) "Out of the Garden" (10-11).
God's Story ♥ "The Snake Trick" (5-6).	*Adam and His Kin* ♦ Chapter 3 "The Punishment."	*Adam and His Kin* ♦ Chapter 3 "The Punishment."
Amazing Expedition Bible ♥ "A Snake in the Grass" (22-23).	*The Victor Journey Through the Bible* ♥ "The Fall" (12).	*The Victor Journey Through the Bible* ♥ "The Fall" (12).
	Genesis: Finding Our Roots ♦ Unit 2 "Book of Adam."	*Genesis: Finding Our Roots* ♦ Unit 2 "Book of Adam."
		An Historical Survey of the Old Testament ★ "The Fall of Man" (56-58).

Internet Sources

Adam and Eve are Tempted
Description: Children's Bible study with puzzles and coloring page in Acrobat file.
http://www.calvarychapel.org/children/site/pdf/Old/Curr004.pdf

An Internet-Linked Unit Study

ⓘ *The Fall of Humankind*
Description: Part of "God's Story: From Creation to Eternity" from ChristianAnswers.net. (Follow the "next" buttons on the bottom of each page.)
http://www.christiananswers.net/godstory/fall1.html

ⓘ *The Fall of Man*
Description: An excellent study, part of "Old Testament Bible Study of the Creation to Abraham Genesis 1 to Genesis 12."
http://bible-truth.org/GEN3.HTM

ⓘ *Genesis 3*
Description: Matthew Henry's Commentary on Genesis 3
http://www.searchgodsword.org/com/mhc-com/view.cgi?book=ge&chapter=3

ⓘ *Genesis 3*
Description: Commentary on Genesis 3 from *The 1599 Geneva Study Bible*.
http://www.searchgodsword.org/com/gsb/view.cgi?book=ge&chapter=003

Step 3: Expand

Choose and complete one of the following activities:

Activity 1: Create a Storyboard
A storyboard is a graphic, sequential depiction of a narrative. Gather the materials you would need to tell the story of the Fall. You can either draw this story or cut out pictures to tell this story to your family and friends. Refer to storyboard directions at
http://homeschoolunitstudies.com/TG/teacherhelps/story.htm

Activity 2: Copy Verses
Copy, by hand or typing, two or more verses about the Fall of Man: Gen. 3:1–19; 2:16,17; Job 31:33; Eccl. 7:29; Isaiah 43:27; Hos. 6:7; Rom. 5:12,14,18,19,21; 1 Corinthians 15:21,22; 2 Cor. 11:3; or 1 Tim. 2:14.

Activity 3: Create a Chart
Create a chart (similar to the chart on the next page) showing the three forms of temptation and subsequent sin: Lust of the Eye, Lust of the Flesh, and The Pride of Life. Re-read Scripture passages about Adam and Eve's temptations, and notice how each of these forms are present in the first sin.

Read John 3:13–17.

Notice that there are three types of application for the Tree of the Knowledge of Good and Evil:

1. A tree that was good for food (natural food for the physical body)

Recommended in: ♦ several lessons in a unit; ★ several units in a volume; ♥ several volumes. ⊙— Key Resource for this unit.

Heart of Wisdom Publishing

Adam to Abraham

    2. A tree that was pleasant to the eyes (carnal food for the mind)
    3. A tree desirable to make one wise (spiritual food)

God's response to these sins shows both judgment and mercy: It shows judgment because Adam and Eve were separated from the close relationship they had enjoyed with God; it shows mercy because God did not let Adam and Eve live forever in this separated state, but gave a way of redemption (read Genesis 3:21). God made a way for all men to return to a relationship with Him. God's first sacrifice was from among His animals, which provided the skins He gave to Adam and Eve to "cover" their "shame," i.e., to cover their sin. God finally gave His Son as the last sacrifice. Discuss with a family member what "paid in full" means. Discuss what this means to you.

Sin	Lust of the Eye	Lust of the Flesh	Pride of Life
Eating from the Tree (disobeying God)	X	X	X
Stealing			
Murder			
Adultery			
Disobeying Parents			

Activity 4: Rewrite a Passage
Henry Thiessen wrote: "The thought is something like this. At first God and man stood face to face with each other in perfect harmony. In sinning, Adam turned his back upon God. . . . Christ's death has satisfied the demands of God and now God has again turned his face toward man. It remains for man to turn around and face God. Since God has been reconciled by the death of his Son, man is now entreated to be reconciled to God." Rewrite this passage in your own words.

Activity 5: Complete Worksheets
Complete *The Serpent's Lie* worksheets and puzzles.
http://www.calvarychapel.org/children/site/pdf/Old/Curr004.pdf

Activity 6: Learn Hebrew Words
The three primary words for *sin* in the Hebrew language are all used in Psalm 51. They are:
    Hata' - to miss the mark, or to fall short of the divine standard.
    Pesa - rebellion or transgression, indicating revolt against the standard. *Awon* - iniquity or guilt, as a twisting of the standard or deviation from it.
    http://bible.crosswalk.com/Lexicons/OldTestamentHebrew/

Activity 7: Discuss
Have you ever faced a strong temptation? What did you do? Did you walk away or succumb? Satan focused Eve's attention upon a specific thing. He made her focus on what she didn't have, when all around her was paradise. He determines the time of the temptation. He waits for our vulnerable moments. His ultimate strategy is to destroy us. He

can't do that, but he can destroy our joy, peace, contentment, and assurance if we allow him to do it. Discuss different temptations in your life. Are there any that occur over and over? Read Eph. 6:10–14. Discuss what you can do next time you are tempted.

 Activity 7: Discuss and Answer Questions

1. Why did God tell Adam and Eve not to eat of the tree?
2. Who is the serpent?
3. What type of lies did the serpent tell Eve?
4. Why did Eve believe the serpent?
5. What did Eve do after she ate from the tree?
6. What did Adam do after he ate from the tree?
7. What curses were put upon man for his disobedience?
8. What curses were put upon woman for her disobedience?
9. What curses were put upon the serpent for his disobedience?
10. What does *enmity* mean?
11. What were the consequences in their relationship with God and their ability to find fulfillment in life?
12. What temporal sacrifice did God provide for their sin?
13. Was there any disease, suffering, or death before the fall?
14. How did Adam and Eve try to deny their guilt?
15. How does this story teach us about how God relates to His people and how they are to relate to Him?
16. How do the cherubim and flaming sword fit into this story?
17. What ultimate sacrifice was provided for all sin?

Step 4: Excel

❏ Correct all written work to demonstrate correct punctuation and spelling.
❏ Correct all written work to demonstrate correct and effective use of grammar.
❏ Add to your Writing Notebook the rules for all punctuation and grammar errors you corrected.
❏ Record any misspelled words in your Spelling Notebook.
❏ Add to your Vocabulary Notebook any new words encountered in this lesson. Include a definition for each word. Use each vocabulary term in a sentence orally or in writing.
❏ Add corrected written work or any illustrations to your Portfolio.
❏ Add any important people or events to your Time Line Book.
❏ Share with a friend or family member an activity you completed for this lesson. Explain to them what you have learned.

Footnote:
1. Henry, M. (1991). *Matthew Henry's Commentary on the Whole Bible* (Ge 3:1). Hendrickson: Peabody.

Adam to Abraham

Cain and Abel H10106

Step 1: Excite

The Narrated Bible 6–8

The story of Cain and Abel is told in Genesis chapter 4. Here were two children brought up in the same home, under absolutely identical circumstances, with the same background, the same teaching concerning the true God, etc., and yet their lives turned out so differently.

Two sacrifices were made. Abel made a sacrifice of the firstborn of his flock, while Cain made a sacrifice of the fruit of the ground. Why do you think one sacrifice was acceptable to God and the other was not? What part did faith play in Cain's and Abel's sacrifices?

Cain was the firstborn. Can you think of other instances in the Bible in which the firstborn son is superseded by the second-born son? (Find the answers in Gen. 17:19–21, Gen. 25:23, Gen. 48:15–20; Ex. 7:1,2.)

Step 2: Examine

Easton's Bible Dictionary says,

> Cain was the firstborn son of Adam and Eve (Genesis chapter 4). He became a tiller of the ground, while his brother Abel followed the pursuits of pastoral life. Cain was "a sullen, self-willed, haughty, vindictive man; wanting the religious element in his character, and defiant even in his attitude towards God." It came to pass *"in process of time"* "at the end of days," (i.e., probably on the Sabbath), that the two brothers presented their offerings to the Lord. Abel's offering was of the *"firstlings of his flock and of the fat,"* while Cain's was *"of the fruit of the ground."* Abel's sacrifice was *"more excellent"* (Hebrews 11:4) than Cain's, and was accepted by God. On this account Cain was *"very wroth,"* and cherished feelings of murderous hatred against his brother, and was at length guilty of the desperate outrage of putting him to death* (1 John 3:12). For this crime he was expelled from Eden [out from the presence of the LORD...Ge 4:16] and henceforth led the life of an exile, bearing upon him some mark which God had set upon him in answer to his own cry for mercy, so that thereby he might be protected from the wrath of his fellow men; or it may be that God only gave him some sign to assure him that he would not be slain (Genesis 4:15).
>
> Doomed to be a wanderer and a fugitive in the earth, he went forth into the "land of Nod," i.e., the land of "exile", which is said to have been in the "east of Eden," and there he built a city, the first we read of, and called it after his son's name, Enoch. His descendants are enumerated to the sixth generation. They gradually degenerated in their moral and spiritual condition until they became wholly corrupt before God. This corruption prevailed, and at length the Deluge was sent by God to prevent the final triumph of evil.[1]

Cain's character continued in his descendants. Four generations later, Lamech was a polygamist (Gen. 4:17–19; compare 2:24). Lamech was also a murderer and wrongly expected God's grace (Gen. 4:23–24).

Suggested Resources

If you would like to know more about Cain and Abel, explore any of the resources listed below.

K-3	4-8	9-12
Read about the Cain and Abel in Genesis. 4:1–16. Also read Heb. 11:4; 1 John 3:12; and Jude 1:11. If you are using the *Narrated Bible* ♥ Read pages 7-8. Also read verses listed above (1651, 1659, 1630).		
Discovering Jesus in Genesis ♦ "Murder Near Paradise" (12-13).	*Discovering Jesus in Genesis* ♦ "Murder Near Paradise" (12-13).	*Discovering Jesus in Genesis* ♦ "Murder Near Paradise" (12-13).
Who's Who in the Bible ♥ "First People of Genesis" (6-7).	*Who's Who in the Bible* ♥ "First People of Genesis" (6-7).	*Who's Who in the Bible* ♥ "First People of Genesis" (6-7).
God's Story ♥ "The Snake Trick" (5-6).	*Adam and His Kin* ♦ Chapter 5 "Cain."	*Adam and His Kin* ♦ Chapter 5 "Cain."
	Genesis: Finding Our Roots ♦ Unit II "The Book of Adam."	*Genesis: Finding Our Roots* ♦ Unit II "The Book of Adam."
	The Victor Journey Through the Bible ♥ "Cain and Abel" (13).	*The Victor Journey Through the Bible* ♥ "Cain and Abel" (13).
	Reproducible Maps, Charts, Timelines & Illustrations ♥ (13).	*Reproducible Maps, Charts, Timelines & Illustrations* ♥ (13).
		An Historical Survey of the Old Testament ★ "The Genealogy of Adam and Eve" (58-60).
		Old Testament Bible History ★ Chapter 2 "Cain and Abel: The Two Ways and the Two Races."

Video

Mysteries of the Bible: Cain and Abel
Description: Their story is one of the most chilling in the Bible: a tale of cold-blooded murder between the world's first brothers. But while Genesis records the identity of Abel's killer, the world's first death remains, in essence, a mystery. What compelled Cain to kill his

Recommended in: ♦ several lessons in a unit; ★ several units in a volume; ♥ several volumes. ☚ Key Resource for this unit.

Adam to Abraham

only brother? How did he do it? Did Cain realize that he was capable of ending Abel's life? And what of the strange paradoxes in the Scripture, eg, Cain's fear of strangers in an unpopulated world and the sudden appearance of a future wife? In this fascinating investigation, modern scholars work like detectives, searching for clues in the seventeen verses that describe humanity's first tragic crime, and explore its ultimate message of resiliency and hope. 50 minutes. Watch local listings for *The History Channel's* viewing time, or order the video (available in some public libraries).
http://store.aetv.com/html/catalog/vp01.jhtml?id=11631

Internet Sources

The Birth of Cain and Abel
Description: An excellent study, part of *Old Testament: Bible Study of the Creation to Abraham, Genesis 1 to Genesis 12.*
http://bible-truth.org/GEN4.HTM

The Broken Family of Cain and Abel
Description: Part 10 of *God's Story: From Creation to Eternity* from ChristianAnswers.net.
http://www.christiananswers.net/godstory/family1.html

Cain and Abel: The Two Ways and the Two Races
Description: Chapter 2 from *Bible History: Old Testament* by Alfred Edersheim.
http://philologos.org/__eb-bhot/vol_I/ch02.htm

Step 3: Expand

Choose and complete one of the following activities:

Activity 1: Write a Description
Faith plays a vital role in the lives of God's people. God kept the covenants made founded on His faithfulness. It is God's faithfulness that should be the guide for our faithfulness. Read Rom. 3:25–30. Use a Bible concordance, topical Bible, or other Bible reference, and describe in one or two paragraphs some of the aspects of God's faithfulness. (Younger students may dictate the description.)

Activity 2: Contrast and Compare
Just as the "best fruit" of Cain would not please God, neither will the sinner's best works get him or her into heaven. God only accepted one offering—the blood sacrifice of Abel. Make a contrast-and-compare graphic comparing Abel's offering with Jesus, the Lamb of God. Visit the URL below for instructions. http://homeschoolunitstudies.com/TG/teacher-helps/contrast.htm

An Internet-Linked Unit Study

Activity 3: Add to Your Time Line Book
Add Cain and Abel to the Time Line Book you created in the first lesson. Consider making paper People (see the back of this book) and dressing them with hair and clothes from Bible times. See our web site for ideas.
http://heartofwisdom.com/paperpeople.htm

Activity 4: Create a Storyboard
A storyboard is a graphic, sequential depiction of a narrative. Gather the materials you need to tell the story of Cain and Abel. You can either draw this story or cut out pictures to tell this story to your family and friends. Refer to storyboard directions.
http://homeschoolunitstudies.com/Ancienthistory/storyboard.htm

Activity 5: Write a Summary
Both Cain and Abel brought offerings to God, but their heart attitudes were different. Write and share a paragraph explaining the term "Man looks on the outward appearance, but God looks at the heart." Younger students may dictate or narrate (tell back) what they learned.

Activity 6: Think and Discuss
When Cain murdered Abel, what emotion preceded the act? (Gen. 4:3–7). Anger is perhaps the strongest, and potentially the most destructive, of our emotions. Unbridled anger is the source for many outward acts of violence and inward roots of bitterness; however, anger itself is not sin (Luke 4:28–30; 2 Cor. 12:10; Gal. 5:20). Eph. 4:26 tells us to be angry, but not to sin. When does anger turn into sin? Discuss different ways to deal with anger. What are biblical steps to release it to God and experience His peace?

Activity 7: Complete Worksheets
Complete the *Cain and Abel* worksheets and puzzles.
http://www.calvarychapel.org/children/site/pdf/Old/Curr005.pdf

Step 4: Excel

- ❏ Correct all written work to demonstrate correct punctuation and spelling.
- ❏ Correct all written work to demonstrate correct and effective use of grammar.
- ❏ Add to your Writing Notebook the rules for all punctuation and grammar errors you corrected.
- ❏ Record any misspelled words in your Spelling Notebook.
- ❏ Add to your Vocabulary Notebook any new words encountered in this lesson. Include a definition for each word. Use each vocabulary term in a sentence orally or in writing.
- ❏ Add corrected written work or any illustrations to your Portfolio.
- ❏ Add any important people or events to your Time Line Book.
- ❏ Share with a friend or family member an activity you completed for this lesson. Explain to them what you have learned.

Footnotes:
1. Edersheim, Alfred. *The Bible History Old Testament*, 1876-1887

Recommended in: ♦ several lessons in a unit; ★ several units in a volume; ● several volumes. ○— Key Resource for this unit.

Adam to Abraham

Seth to Noah H10107

Step 1: Excite

The Narrated Bible

Alfred Edersheim wrote in *Bible History: Old Testament,*

> "The place of Abel could not remain unfilled if God's purpose of mercy were to be carried out." Seth was the third son of Adam and Eve mentioned in the Bible. Seth's recorded descendants down to Noah are Enos, Cainan, Mahalaleel, Jared, Enoch, Methuselah, Lamech, and Noah. The Bible is an integrated message system, the product of supernatural engineering. Every number, every place name, every detail, every jot and tittle is there for our learning, our discovery, and our amazement.[1]

There is an exciting message in the names of the descendants of Adam through his son Seth down to Noah! Ray C. Stedman analyzes these names in his book, *Understanding Man*:

> "...a way of escape [for man] is indicated again in a most fascinating way in this chapter by the meaning of the names listed. There is some difference among authorities as to the meaning of these names, depending upon the root from which they are judged to be taken. But one authority gives a most interesting sequence of meanings. The list begins with Seth, which means "Appointed."

Name	Meaning
Seth	Appointed
Enosh	Mortal
Kenan	Sorrow
Mahalalel	The Blessed God
Jared	Came Down
Enoch	Teaching
Methuselah	His death shall bring
Lamech	Strength
Noah	Comfort

God has Appointed that

Mortal man shall Sorrow;

but The Blessed God, Came

Down, Teaching,

that His Death Shall Bring,

Strength and Comfort.

An Internet-Linked Unit Study

Step 2: Examine

Seth means "substituted"or "appointed" Gen. 4:25 says, *And Adam knew his wife again; and she bare a son, and called his name Seth: For God, said she, hath appointed me another seed instead of Abel, whom Cain slew.* While Adam and Eve had more children, it is through Seth that God's promised salvation would come. Read Luke 3:38.

Not much is written about the genealogy from Seth to Abram. We do know certain things about some of these men. For example, we know the ages to which these men lived, and we know what their ages were when they fathered the next in the genealogy.

Suggested Resources

If you would like to know more about the genealogy from Seth to Noah, explore any of the resources listed below.

K-3	4-8	9-12
Read Genesis chapter 5 (Book of generations). As you read take notes of each person listed in order. If you are using the *Narrated Bible* ❤ Read pages 8-10.		
Who's Who in the Bible ❤ Read: "First People of Genesis" (6-7).	*Who's Who in the Bible* ❤ Read: "First People of Genesis" (6-7).	*Who's Who in the Bible* ❤ Read: "First People of Genesis" (6-7).
	Adam and His Kin ♦ Chapters 2- 6.	*Adam and His Kin* ♦ Chapters 2- 6.
	Genesis: Finding Our Roots ♦ Unit II "The Book of Adam."	*Genesis: Finding Our Roots* ♦ Unit II "The Book of Adam."
		Bible History: Old Testament ★ Read: Chapter 3 "Seth and his Descendants - The Race of Cain."

Internet Sources

ⓘ *The Genealogy of the Royal Line from Adam to Noah*
Description: An excellent study, part of *Old Testament Bible Study: Creation to Abraham, Genesis 1 to Genesis 12.*
http://bible-truth.org/GEN5.HTM

ⓘ *Genesis Five*
Description: Verses with commentary on Generations after Adam.
http://www.bibleexplained.com/moses/Gene/ge05.htm

Recommended in: ♦ several lessons in a unit; ★ several units in a volume; ❤ several volumes. ☛ Key Resource for this unit.

Adam to Abraham

Seth and his Descendants - The Race of Cain
Description: Chapter 3 from *Bible History: Old Testament*, by Alfred Edersheim.
http://philologos.org/__eb-bhot/vol_I/ch03.htm

The Stone Age to the Flood to before 2000 BC
Description: MustardSeed Media annotated time line.
http://www.mustardseed.net/timeline/timeline2.html

Step 3: Expand

Activity 1: Make a Family Tree with Paper People
You'll need poster board, card stock or pre-cut paper people figures, a glue stick, and construction paper. Use pre-cut paper people or images from back of this book. Dress and label each figure with a name. Place the figures in chronological order on the poster board telling the story of the genealogy from Adam to Noah. Refer to Genesis chapter 5.
http://heartofwisdom.com/paperpeople.htm

Activity 2: Add to Your Time Line Book
Using the ages mentioned in Genesis, make a time line of the lives of each of the men in the genealogy chain from Adam to Noah. Add this time line to your Time Line Book.

Activity 3: Complete Worksheets
Fill out the worksheets on Enoch from the URL below, which includes puzzles, coloring pages and a fill-in-the-blank sheet.
http://www.calvarychapel.org/children/site/pdf/Old/Curr006.pdf

Step 4: Excel

☐ Correct all written work to demonstrate correct punctuation and spelling.
☐ Correct all written work to demonstrate correct and effective use of grammar.
☐ Add to your Writing Notebook the rules for all punctuation and grammar errors you corrected.
☐ Record any misspelled words in your Spelling Notebook.
☐ Add to your Vocabulary Notebook any new words encountered in this lesson. Include a definition for each word. Use each vocabulary term in a sentence orally or in writing.
☐ Add corrected written work or any illustrations to your Portfolio.
☐ Add any important people or events to your Time Line Book.
☐ Share with a friend or family member an activity you completed for this lesson. Explain to them what you have learned.

Footnotes
1. Missler Chuck, *Cosmic Codes: Hidden Messages from the Edge of Eternity*, Koinonia House, 1999.
2. Edersheim, Alfred. *The Bible History Old Testament*, 1876-1887
3. Stedman, Ray C. *Understanding Man; How We Got to Where We Are*, Questar Publishers, 1986.

An Internet-Linked Unit Study

Corruption of Man H10108
Pre flood - Antediluvian

The Narrated Bible

Step 1: Excite

Adam and Eve are good but immature, fine but breakable like glass dishes. They are without flaw, yet capable of marring themselves. Satan as a serpent to tempts Eve, first to question God, then to rebel against Him. First Satan introduces doubts about God's authority and goodness: *Did God really say, "You must not eat from any tree in the garden?"* (Gen. 3:1). He invites Eve to consider how the fruit of the Tree of Knowledge is good for food and for knowledge. We see the tendency of sin to begin with a subtle appeal to something attractive and good in itself, to an act that is somehow plausible and directed toward some good end; the first sins disclose the essence of later sins. Sin involves the refusal of humankind to accept its God-given position between the Creator and lower creation. It flows from decisions to reject God's way, and to steal, curse, and lie simply because that seems more attractive or reasonable.[1]

Antediluvian man became very corrupt, so corrupt that God "repented" that He had made man. We may take a superficial look at the corruption of man; however, the corruption of creation caused by sin is far deeper than we can sometimes imagine. All sickness and all disease came from this corruption. The very building blocks of man himself (the DNA) became corrupt.

One of the foundations of the Christian walk is understanding your condition in sin and your need before God. Only then can one appreciate the grace of God in our salvation. Most Christians realize we are saved by God's grace but many do not understand the depth of their sin and the extent of grace that has been given them in their salvation. It is only when we realize how fallen we are that we can realize the degree of grace that has been given to us in our salvation.

Step 2: Examine

Two days before the crucifixion of Christ, His disciples asked Him, *What shall be the sign of thy coming, and of the end of the age?* (Matt. 24:3). His reply pointed to a number of *signs*, all of which together would occur in that generation which would see the signs, and which would be the sign they had requested. These signs climaxed with the prophetic warning, *But as the days of Noe were, so shall also the coming of the Son of Man be. For as in the days that were before the flood they were eating and drinking, marrying and giving in marriage, until the day that Noe entered into the ark, And knew not until the flood came, and took them all away; so shall also the coming of the Son of man be.* (Matt. 24:37–39). Thus did Jesus not only verify the historicity of antediluvian culture and the great Flood, and remind us of the relationship between wickedness and judgment, but He also encouraged us to study closely the characteristics of the days before the Flood, because these would also characterize the days just before His return.[2]

Recommended in: ♦ several lessons in a unit; ★ several units in a volume; ♥ several volumes. ☜ Key Resource for this unit.

Heart of Wisdom Publishing

To corrupt means "to make morally depraved." It means to pervert what is good and upright; it means to make unclean what was once clean. It means to spoil what was once good and unspoiled. The word *corrupt* always implies a former state that was unspoiled, clean, good, or upright. It is never used to speak of the original created nature of man. It speaks of what man has become because of spoiling or perverting the nature with which he was created.[3]

So far in this unit you have seen one failure of man after another, failures that are being repeated today. Adam and Eve disobeyed God and were cast out of the Garden (Genesis chapter 3). Cain murdered his brother Abel (Genesis chapter 4). And now we see humanity is so corrupt that God cleansed the earth with a flood (Genesis chapter 6–8). Sadly the world is no better today. Stories of disobedience, murder, and deception are in news broadcast and even entertainment shows on television every night.

The passage from Romans below explains what happens when man forgets God. When man does not have God in control of his life everything becomes futile or vain. He walks in darkness with no light. Read the passage below slowly at least twice.

> *Although they knew God, they neither glorified Him as God nor gave thanks to Him, but their thinking became futile and their foolish hearts were darkened. Although they claimed to be wise, they became fools and exchanged the glory of the immortal God for images made to look like mortal man and birds and animals and reptiles.*
> *Therefore God gave them over in the sinful desires of their hearts to sexual impurity for the degrading of their bodies with one another. They exchanged the truth of God for a lie, and worshiped and served created things rather than the Creator—who is forever praised. ... Furthermore, since they did not think it worthwhile to retain the knowledge of God, He gave them over to a depraved mind, to do what ought not to be done. They have become filled with every kind of wickedness, evil, greed, and depravity. They are full of envy, murder, strife, deceit, and malice. They are gossips, slanderers, God-haters, insolent, arrogant, and boastful; they invent ways of doing evil; they disobey their parents; they are senseless, faithless, heartless, ruthless. Although they know God's righteous decree that those who do such things deserve death, they not only continue to do these very things, but also approve of those who practice them* (Romans 1:21–25, 8–32).

Genesis chapter 5 lists ten generations from Adam to Noah. Adam lived for 930 years, others each lived for hundreds of years. Some have said that their *years* were much shorter than ours. But the chronology of the Flood (7:11–8:14) shows that Genesis assumes about 360 days in a year. The Sumerian King Lists, lists eight kings who reigned before the Flood for a total of 241,000 years. This makes the 1500 years covered by Genesis 5 seem quite modest.

Enoch lived before the Flood; it is said that he walked with God. He is also one of only two individuals who never died (Elijah - II Kings 2:11). Little is known about him, but the Bible reveals him to be exemplary among men and special to God. He was a man of faith who apparently never died. *By faith Enoch was translated that he should not see death; and was not found, because God had translated him: for before his translation he had this testimony, that he pleased God. But without faith it is impossible to please him: for he that cometh to God must believe that he is, and that he is a rewarder of them that diligently seek him* (Heb. 11:5–6). Enoch had ample faith in the fact and work of God, which yielded a close walk with God. Enoch's faith pleased God.

Suggested Resources

If you would like to know more about life before the Flood, explore any of the resources listed below.

K-3	4-8	9-12
Read Genesis chapter 4 to get a brief glimpse into the society and culture of mankind before the Flood. It describes cities, polygamy, nomadic herdsmen, musical instruments, bronze, and iron. If you are using the *Narrated Bible* ♥ Read pages 11.		
God's Story ♥ Read: "A World Under Water" (6-7).	*Adam and His Kin* ♦ Read: Chapter 8 "Noah" and Chapter 9 "The Year 1656."	*Adam and His Kin* ♦ Read: Chapter 8 "Noah" and Chapter 9 "The Year 1656."
Amazing Expedition Bible ♥ "The Great Flood" (24).	*Genesis: Finding Our Roots* ♦ Read: Unit 3 "Book of Noah."	*Genesis: Finding Our Roots* ♦ Read: Unit 3 "Book of Noah."
		Bible History: Old Testament ★ Read: Chapter 5 "The Universal Corruption of Man - Preparation for the Flood."

Additional Reading:

ⓘ *In the Days of Noah* by Gloria Clanin; Earl and Bonita Snellenberger K-3 4-8
Description: A fictionalized retelling of the story of how Noah and his family followed God's commands and built an ark to protect the animals from a great flood introduces information about creation, life in Noah's times, and the evidence for the historical accuracy of the biblical account. Library Binding: 80 pages, Word Publishing (1996) ISBN: 0890512051.

Internet Sources

ⓘ *The Fall of Man. Genesis 3:1–24*
Description: An excellent study, part of *Old Testament Bible Study: Creation to Abraham, Genesis 1 to Genesis 12*.
http://bible-truth.org/GEN3.HTM

ⓘ *The Population of the Pre-Flood World*
Description: Chapter 5 from *Bible History: Old Testament*, by Alfred Edersheim.
http://philologos.org/__eb-bhot/vol_I/ch05.htm

ⓘ *Sin, Repentance and Forgiveness*
Description: An article by Clarence H. Wagner, Jr., from *Israel Teaching Letter*, discussing Christianity's theology of *original sin*, and Judaism's theology that man has the *proclivity to sin*.
http://www.bridgesforpeace.com/publications/teaching/Article-29.html

---

Recommended in: ♦ several lessons in a unit; ★ several units in a volume; ♥ several volumes. ⓞ– Key Resource for this unit.

Adam to Abraham

Step 3: Expand

Choose and complete one of the following activities:

Activity 1: Write a Description
Write a description of society and culture of mankind before the Flood using the verses in Genesis 4. Younger students may dictate the description.

Activity 2: Copy
Copy Romans 1:21–25 and 28–32 listed in Step 2.

Activity 3: Write an Article
Look at today's newspaper or listen to a news broadcast. What do you think is God's reaction to the stories in that paper or on that broadcast? Pick out one story and try to see what God sees. Write an article explaining what you think God feels, and what you think our response should be to God's reaction.

Activity 4: Expand Research
Find out about the four major theological theories on original sin. These theories did not exist until about the third century A.D., and there was no generally accepted doctrine until the fifth century A.D.[4]

1. The Wesleyan (also called Mediate Imputation or Theory of Condemnation for Depravity) view states that we inherit corruption (sin nature) from Adam, but not actual sin.
2. The Augustinian view came from Augustine (also called the Theory of Adam's Natural Headship or the Realistic Theory). He believed that we were actually present in Adam when he sinned, which is how we can be held guilty for what he did.
3. The Federal Theory (also called Immediate Imputation) says that God holds us guilty of the same sin Adam committed, from the moment we are born.
4. The Pelagian belief is that there is no original sin, and that we are responsible for our own sin only. This is the theological doctrine propounded by Pelagius, a British monk, who believed that humans can merit heaven by leading righteous lives.

Whether you believe in theology of *original sin*, or that man has the *proclivity to sin*, the bottom line is the same: man can, and does, sin against God. Humans are not animals, and because we have understanding and moral consciousness, we are responsible for our actions, which have consequences. We know from the Bible, that the *wages of sin is death* (Rom. 6:23), which effectively separates us from God, now and in eternity. Deut. 24:16 makes it clear that *each* [person] *is to die for his own sin*. This death has both spiritual and physical dimensions, and no one can escape paying the price.[5] To find out more on this topic see: *Are Men Born Sinners? The Myth of Original Sin.* An online book written by A. T. Overstreet. http://www.gospeltruth.net/menbornsinners/mbsindex.htm

Step 4: Excel

- ❏ Correct all written work to demonstrate correct punctuation and spelling.
- ❏ Correct all written work to demonstrate correct and effective use of grammar.
- ❏ Add to your Writing Notebook the rules for all punctuation and grammar errors you corrected.
- ❏ Record any misspelled words in your Spelling Notebook.
- ❏ Add to your Vocabulary Notebook any new words encountered in this lesson. Include a definition for each word. Use each vocabulary term in a sentence orally or in writing.
- ❏ Add any important people or events to your Time Line Book.
- ❏ Share with a friend or family member an activity you completed for this lesson. Explain to them what you have learned.

Footnotes
1. Elwell, Walter A. 1997. Entry for "Sin", *Evangelical Dictionary of Theology*.
2. Unruh, J. Timothy. 1995. "The Days of Noah and the Sons of God" [online]. Lambert Dolphin's Research Library [Cited August 2002]. Available from World Wide Web: <http://www.ldolphin.org/unruh/giants.html>
3. Overstreet, A. T. "Are Men Born Sinners?" [Cited August 2000]. Available from World Wide Web: <http://www.gospeltruth.net/menbornsinners/mbs04.htm>
4. Wagner, Clarence H., Jr. "Sin, Repentance And Forgiveness," "Israel Teaching Letter." Bridges For Peace.][Cited December 2002]. Available from World Wide Web: <http://bridgesforpeace.com>
5. The focus of the activity is not to determine the theory of original sin. It is to show students that many doctrines accepted as biblical fact actually came into existence years after the Bible was written.

Adam to Abraham

The Flood H10109

Step 1: Excite

The Narrated Bible

Noah found grace in the eyes of the Lord. (Gen 6:8) Noah was a righteous man, blameless among the people of his time, and he walked with God. Can you imagine being Noah when God told him He was going to put an end to all mortals on earth? Can you imagine being the only righteous person living in a spiritual and moral wasteland? How do you think Noah *found grace in the eyes of the Lord*? Some translations say Noah found favor in the eyes of the Lord. The words grace or favor in this verse means *acts which display one's compassion for another; be pleased, be favorably disposed, formally,* and/or *be good in the eyes*.[1]

It took Noah and his sons approximately 120 years to build the ark. Go on a field trip to get an idea of the size of the ark. You'll need to find a four or five story building. This will give you an idea of the ark's height. Next go to a football field, the ark was one and half times this length. Finally observe a six lane highway to get an idea of the width. Now imagine working on this boat daily for well over a hundred years 500 miles or more away from the closest body of water? Can you imagine the public ridicule?

As you study this lesson, think about your life. Are you willing to do things God's way rather than your own? Are you willing to trust God's ability rather than your agenda?

Step 2: Examine

The Genesis account of the Flood of Noah is very specific. The Flood lasted 371 days, it was not just a local flood. The Hebrew word used *kataklusmos* means "cataclysm" and is applied only to the Genesis Flood. It is clear that this yearlong flood, some six miles of water, produced dramatic desolation. Indeed, it must have been a catastrophic event. The flood was extensive enough to wipe out all living humans on earth except the eight persons who were on board the ark (Gen 7:23; 1 Pet 3:20). Genesis 6:17 clearly says that the flood destroyed all life under the heavens—except, of course, the fish and the eight people aboard on the Ark.

Noah's Ark, constitutes the one remaining archaeological link to the world before the Flood. No other major antediluvian artifact is likely ever to be found.[1] In Matt. 24:37–39 Jesus uses the account of the universal Flood and its destruction to point to His second coming and judgment, which is also a universal event. As in the days of Noah, when all who were outside the ark were destroyed, so it will be at he coming of the Son of Man, when all those outside the ark of safety, Jesus Christ (those who have not accepted Him as Savior), shall be judged and condemned.

In Step One, we discussed the huge size of the ark. How many animals were on the ark? Would two of all animals and seven of all clean animals fit in a boat?

An Internet-Linked Unit Study

John Whitcomb and Henry Morris, in their book, *The Genesis Flood*, did an exceptionally thorough job of analyzing the pertinent data relating to the physical dimensions and carrying capacity of the ark. They note that the ark would have been 437.5 feet in length, 72.92 feet in width, and 43.75 feet in height (figuring from 17.5 inches per cubit). Calculating for two of each on the ark, there would need to be room for only 35,200 animals, plus five each of clean animals (a very small number, but for the sake of argument, allow for half the species or 8,800 x 5 being 44,000), a total of 79,000 animals maximum would have been on the Ark.

Suggested Resources

To learn more about the Flood, explore any of the resources listed below.

K-3	4-8	9-12
Read about Noah and the flood in Genesis chapters 6-8. If you are using the *Narrated Bible* ♥ Read pages 12-15.		
Discovering Jesus in Genesis ♦ "The Flood" (14-15).	*Discovering Jesus in Genesis* ♦ "The Flood" (14-15).	*Discovering Jesus in Genesis* ♦ "The Flood" (14-15).
God's Story ♥ "A World Under Water" (6-7)	*Nelson's Illustrated Encyclopedia of the Bible* ♥⚷ "Genesis " (198-199)	*Nelson's Illustrated Encyclopedia of the Bible* ♥⚷ "Genesis " (198-199)
The Victor Journey Through the Bible ♥ "Noah Builds the Ark" (14-15)	*The Victor Journey Through the Bible* ♥ "Noah Builds the Ark" (14-15)	*The Victor Journey Through the Bible* ♥ "Noah Builds the Ark" (14-15)
Amazing Expedition Bible ♥ "The Great Flood" (24-27).	*Amazing Expedition Bible* ♥ "The Great Flood" (24-27).	*The Holman Bible Atlas* ♥ "Introduction" (2).
Who's Who in the Bible ♥ "First People of Genesis" (6-7), "Abraham and His People" (8-9)	*Who's Who in the Bible* ♥ "First People of Genesis" (6-7), "Abraham and His People" (8-9)	*The Bible Comes Alive: Volume One, Creation to Abraham* ★ Section I "Early Genesis Is Factual History."
		An Historical Survey of the Old Testament ★ "In the Beginning" (45-72).

Additional Books

The Genesis Flood by Henry M. Morris and John C. Whitcomb 9-12
Description: This is the book that many recognize as having started the modern revival of creationism and catastrophism. Although it has gone through over thirty-two printings, it is still the most definitive treatment of the biblical and scientific evidence of the global flood in the days of Noah. Paperback. P & R Press; (1989) ISBN: 0875523382.

Recommended in: ♦ several lessons in a unit; ★ several units in a volume; ♥ several volumes. ⚷ Key Resource for this unit.

Heart of Wisdom Publishing

Adam to Abraham

Grand Canyon: Monument to Catastrophe by Steven A. Austin 9-12
Description: True science will not disagree with God. This means that we must always test the so-called sciences in the light of truth. For example, evolution would tell you that species evolved into higher forms of life. However, science also tells you that the universe is in a state of decline. Both cannot be true, and since the latter position is provable by consistent laboratory example, the first must be false. Paperback. (September 1995) Institute for Creation Research; ISBN: 0932766331.

Internet Sources

The Ark of Salvation
Description: Excellent Bible study comparing the Ark to Christ.
http://www.abideinchrist.org/messages/gen6v14.html

The Great Flood Begins
Description: Portion of *Old Testament Bible Study: Creation to Abraham, Genesis 1 to Genesis 12.*
http://bible-truth.orgy/GEN7.HTM

Why Does Nearly Every Culture Have a Tradition of a Global Flood?
Description: John D. Morris, Ph.D. from the Institute for Creation Research explains that one of the strongest evidences for the global flood which annihilated all people on earth except for Noah and his family, has been the ubiquitous presence of flood legends in the folklore of people groups from around the world.
http://www.icr.org/pubs/btg-b/btg-153b.htm

The Flood of Noah and the Epic of Gligamesh
Description: Frank Lorey, M. A. from the Institute for Creation Research explains the popular theory proposed by liberal *scholars*, that the Hebrews *borrowed* from the Babylonians, has no conclusive proof. The differences, including religious, ethical, and sheer quantity of details, make it unlikely that the Biblical account was dependent on any extant source from the Sumerian traditions. Instead, the Epic of Gilgamesh contains the corrupted account as preserved and embellished by peoples who did not follow the God of the Hebrews.
http://www.icr.org/pubs/imp/imp-285.htm

Noah and the Great Flood
Description: Part of "God's Story: From Creation to Eternity" from ChristianAnswers.net. (Follow the "next" buttons on the bottom of each page.)
http://www.christiananswers.net/godstory/flood1.html

From Where Came the Extra Water for the Great Flood?
Description: Explanation of the earth's water sources before and during the Flood, from God's point of view. http://www.godspointofview.com/public/answers/extra water.html

An Internet-Linked Unit Study

Grand Canyon: Startling Evidence for Noah's Flood!
Description: A careful examination of the evidence, backed up by experiments and observations of processes operating today, indicates catastrophic deposition of sand by deep, fast-moving water in a matter of days, totally consistent with conditions envisaged during the Flood.
http://www.answersingenesis.org/home/area/magazines/docs/v15n1_grandcanyon.asp

TV and Videos

Biography: Noah
Every school child knows the story of Noah's Ark and how he brought the world's animals on board "two by two." But what do we actually know about Noah the sailor, the vintner, the farmer, the healer, the holy man who is said to have lived for 950 years? This remarkable program creates a complete portrait of Noah, prophet of the Flood, using interviews with experts and historians, film footage from the Holy Land, and rare paintings and artifacts. Watch your local *A&E* schedule for viewing times, or order the video online.
http://store.aetv.com/html/catalog/vp01.jhtml?id=14114

History's Mysteries: The Search For Noah's Ark
Description: Biblical archaeologists have uncovered sufficient evidence to support claims that some parts of the Bible, at least, are based on fact. But proof supporting the story of Noah and his famous ark remain elusive. Guided by a host of experts, including the editor of *The Oxford Encyclopedia of Archeology*, this program examines the most intriguing theories, discoveries, and claims. Interest level: junior high/adult. Watch your local *A&E* schedule for viewing times, or order the video online.
http://store.aetv.com/html/catalog/vp01.jhtml?id=43175

The Quest for Noah's Ark
Description: High atop a mountain in Eastern Turkey is a 5,000 year old wooden ship. Is it Noah's Ark? Did the biblical story of Noah and the Flood actually happen? Has the Ark really been located? New expeditions and scientific investigations using satellites, computers, and aerial spy cameras have provided amazing answers to these questions. "Winner of the Dove Family Approved Seal Award" (Publisher's description).
http://www.christianbook.com/Christian/Books/product?event=AFF&p=1012868&item_no=679546

The World That Perished: Evidence of the Global Flood of Genesis
Description: Combines special-effects animation with other outstanding visuals. Brings to light the scientific and historic evidence that God's judgment—Noah's Flood—was both real and global. Reveals the fascinating facts and planet-changing nature of the Flood. Biblically accurate, it answers the doubts of skeptics and strongly strengthens faith in the Bible. Available from Paradise Gardens: (800) 332-2261, or online at: http://www.christiananswers.net/catalog/wp-vs.html

---

Recommended in: ♦ several lessons in a unit; ★ several units in a volume; ● several volumes. ☞ Key Resource for this unit.

Step 3: Expand

Choose and complete one of the following activities:

Activity 1: Contrast and Compare
Compare man's wickedness in the days of Noah with that of today. Watch television and notice how many times God's commandments are broken or ridiculed in a typical comedy or drama. Make a contrast-and-compare graphic. Visit the URL below for instructions. http://homeschoolunitstudies.com/TG/teacherhelps/contrast.htm

Activity 2: Add to Your Time Line Book
Add the story of the Flood to your Time Line Book.

Activity 3: Draw the Dimensions of the Ark
The dimensions of the Ark are given in *cubits in* Genesis 6:13-16 . A cubit was the distance from a man's elbow to the tip of his fingers; generally about eighteen inches. Draw the dimensions of the Ark on graph paper making the scale 18 inches = 1 cubit.

Activity 4: Make a Scrapbook Page
Create a scrapbook page showing Noah building the Ark or the Ark floating on water. Look through coloring books or the Internet for Ark or rainbow images. Use Paper People in the back of this book to create Noah's family. Get creative; consider a fish, ocean or rainbow border, adding animal stickers, lettering, journaling Bible verses on a section of the page, etc. Send us a photo or scan of your page to share with others.
See sample pages at http://HeartofWisdom.com/studentswork.htm.

Activity 5: Answer Questions
Answer the following:
1. How was the Flood foretold? (Gen. 6:13,17)
2. Was does the New Testament say about the Flood? (Matt. 24:38; Luke 17:26,27; Heb. 11:7; 1 Pet. 3:20; 2 Pet. 2:5)
3. What promise did God make? (Gen. 8:20,21; Isa. 54:9)
4. How was Noah in the spiritual wilderness like Jesus in the physical wilderness?

Activity 6: Write an Article
Floods are one of the most deadly and damaging natural disasters known to mankind. The amount of power in even a relatively small flood is staggering. In 1931, the Huang He River in China flooded, making eighty million people homeless, and killing over one million people. Imagine that you are writing for a newspaper. Using the results of your research, write an article (minimum 250 words) about flooding. Compare the different types of floods and the damage they can cause. As you will see from your research, even localized floods cause millions, possibly billions, of dollars of damage each year. Be aware that the total sum of all floods in the world can be considered minor when compared to the great Flood. Use the encyclopedia, news articles, or other sources.

Activity 7: Write a Paper
From your research, write a paper titled "Arguments for a Universal Flood." Hints: the depth (Genesis 7:19–20), the duration, New Testament references (2 Peter 3:6–7), and size of the ark.

Activity 8: Build a Scale Model of the Ark
Build a model from 3/4 inch white pine or 1/2 inch particle board. Refer to instructions at *Building a Scale Model of Noah's Ark at* http://www.icr.orgy/pubs/imp/imp-322.htm

Activity 9: Do a Word Study
God said to Noah what He said to Adam and Eve, *Be fruitful, and multiply*. Some read these verses as a command which in Hebrew can be just as easily interpreted as a blessing. Use a Bible lexicon and look up the words *fruitful* and *multiply*. *And God blessed Noah and his sons, and said unto them, Be fruitful, and multiply, and replenish the earth*. (Gen 9:1).

Step 4: Excel

- ❏ Correct all written work to demonstrate correct punctuation and spelling.
- ❏ Correct all written work to demonstrate correct and effective use of grammar.
- ❏ Add to your Writing Notebook the rules for all punctuation and grammar errors you corrected.
- ❏ Record any misspelled words in your Spelling Notebook.
- ❏ Add to your Vocabulary Notebook any new words encountered in this lesson. Include a definition for each word. Use each vocabulary term in a sentence orally or in writing.
- ❏ Add corrected written work or any illustrations to your Portfolio.
- ❏ Add any important people or events to your Time Line Book.
- ❏ Share with a friend or family member an activity you completed for this lesson. Explain to them what you have learned.

Footnotes
1. Whitcomb, John and Morris,Henry. 1989, *The Genesis Flood,* P & R Press, Nashua, NH
2. Swanson, J. 1997. Dictionary of Biblical Languages with Semantic Domains: Hebrew (Old Testament) (HGK2834). Logos Research Systems, Inc.: Oak Harbo3. Morris, John. 1975. "Noah's Ark Status" [online]. Institute of Creation Research, "Vital Articles on Science/Creation" [Cited 11, 2001]. Available from World Wide Web: <http://www.icr.orgy/pubs/imp/imp-022.htm>

Recommended in: ♦ several lessons in a unit; ★ several units in a volume; ● several volumes. ☚ Key Resource for this unit.

Adam to Abraham

After the Flood H10110

The Narrated Bible 14–16

Step 1: Excite

After the Flood, nothing was the same; nothing was left unchanged. The earth had been cleansed. Aside from Noah and his sons and their wives, not only was man gone, so was everything else. However, even after the terrible flood waters changed the earth forever, God showed mercy.

As mankind spread around the globe, many people began herding and farming. People had the option of increasing food production through work. Africa, America, and Australia had a few large mammals that could be domesticated for farming.

Step 2: Examine

In *Knowing God through Genesis*, David Egne explains how we can see God through the Flood:

> In God's grief over man's wickedness, we see the disappointment of a loving God who desires our best. In His destruction of the human race, we see the wrath of God poured out on disobedience. In the singling out of Noah for rescue, we see a sovereign God who cares for individuals. In the shimmering rainbow, we see an unending reminder that God keeps His word.[1]

Egne also explains that we can see ourselves through the Flood:

> In the unrestrained evil of the race, we see our own pattern of sin before God's grace transformed us. In the refusal of Noah's neighbors to heed his preaching, we see our own resistance to God's spokesmen for justice and truth. In the faith and obedience of Noah, we are given a model for our own relationship with the Lord. In the new beginning for mankind after leaving the ark, we see reflected our own opportunities to start afresh with God.

And Noah lived after the flood three hundred and fifty years. And all the days of Noah were nine hundred and fifty years: and he died (Gen. 9:28–29). After the Flood, Noah built an altar to God (Gen. 8:20) and made a sacrifice. God accepted the sacrifice (Gen. 8:21) and promised Noah that He would never destroy the world again with a flood (Gen. 9:15). The rainbow is the sign of His promise (Gen. 9:12–17). God told Noah to "*be fruitful, and multiply, and fill the earth*" (Gen. 9:1); the same words He had spoken to Adam in Gen. 1:28.

The "Noachide laws" were given after the Flood to Noah for all mankind. God's rainbow was put in the clouds as the sign of His covenant with Noah, and was His pledge that never again would He destroy all flesh by a flood. Rainbows are referred to three other times in Scripture (Ezek. 1:27,28; Rev. 4:1–3; 10:1). Some believe that the rainbow was formed by the change in atmospheric conditions caused by dropping of the water canopy. When we see a rainbow, it should prompt us to think of more than light bending—it should remind us of God's mercy and grace.

The rainbow and its seven colors serve as a visual reminder of our obligation, to observe the Seven Laws of Noah:

1. Do not worship idols.
2. Do not blaspheme.
3. Do not murder.
4. Do not have immoral relations.
5. Do not steal.
6. Properly respect all living animals.
7. Set up courts of law.

The U.S. Congress officially recognized the Noachide laws in legislation which was passed by both houses in 1991. Congress and the President of the United States at that time, George Bush, indicated in Public Law 102–14, 102nd Congress, that the United States of America was founded upon the Seven Universal Laws of Noah, and that these Laws have been the bedrock of society from the dawn of civilization. They also acknowledged that the Seven Laws of Noah are the foundation upon which civilization stands, that recent weakening of these principles threaten the fabric of civilized society, and that justified preoccupation in educating the Citizens of the United States of America and future generations is needed. For this purpose, this Public Law designated March 26, 1991 as Education Day, U.S.A.[2]

In the foreword of *The Spirit of the Law* by Ron Moseley, Roy Blizzard wrote:

> The underlying idea of law, as it is used in the Bible, is that of teaching and instruction. Law is God instructing His people that they may know how to live in a moral and ethical way, pleasing unto Him, and at peace with our fellow man. Law is instruction that, if followed, will enrich one's life, if ignored will diminish it. Law was for the purpose of instructing man how he was to live here in this world. . . The idea of Law in Hebrew is not something that, if transgressed, is going to get you zapped.[2]

The Things God Has Planned

It's sometimes very difficult
For us to understand
The wisdom and the love behind
The things that God has planned.

But we wouldn't have the rainbow
If we didn't have the rain;
We wouldn't know of pleasure
If we never tasted pain.

We wouldn't love the sunrise
If we hadn't felt the night;
And we wouldn't know our weakness
If we hadn't sensed God's might.

We couldn't have the springtime
Or the yellow daffodil
If we hadn't first experienced
The winter's frosty chill.

And though the brilliant sunshine
Is something God had made
He knew too much could parch our souls
So He created shade.

So God's given us a balance:
Enough joys to keep us glad,
Enough tears to keep us humble,
Enough good to balance bad.

And if you'll trust in Him you'll see
Though yesterday brought sorrow,
The clouds will part and dawn will bring
A happier tomorrow.

Source unknown

Adam to Abraham

Suggested Resources

To learn more about time after the Flood, explore any of the resources listed below.

K-3	4-8	9-12
Read Gen. 8:6–20. Then read Gen 9:1–7. These verses describe what is said to be the first form of government. If you are using the *Narrated Bible* ♥ Read pages 16-17.		
Discovering Jesus in Genesis ♦ "The Promise of Protection: The Rainbow"(16-17).	*Discovering Jesus in Genesis* ♦ "The Promise of Protection: The Rainbow"(16-17).	*Discovering Jesus in Genesis* ♦ "The Promise of Protection: The Rainbow"(16-17).
Amazing Expedition Bible ♥ "God's Promise" (27).	*Amazing Expedition Bible* ♥ "God's Promise" (27).	*Amazing Expedition Bible* ♥ "God's Promise" (27).
	Adam and His Kin ♦ Chapter 11 "The Calendar Puzzle" and Chapter 12 "Starting up the New World."	*Adam and His Kin* ♦ Chapter 11 "The Calendar Puzzle" and Chapter 12 "Starting up the New World."
	Genesis: Finding Our Roots ♦ Unit 4 "Book of the Sons of Noah."	*Genesis: Finding Our Roots* ♦ Unit 4 "Book of the Sons of Noah."

Also Recommended

After the Flood by Arthur Geisert K-3 4-8 9-12
Description: This sequel to *The Ark* traces the establishment and development of communities on earth and offers an original theory for events that followed the Great Flood. Geisert's beautiful, full-color etchings alternate between panoramic views and detailed glimpses of everything from the ark to Mount Ararat. "With a stroke of originality, Geisert continues the oft-told tale of the Great Flood by imagining life for Noah and his retinue as the waters begin to recede . . . An understated, quietly powerful book." — Publishers Weekly. Hardcover: 32 pages, Houghton Mifflin Co (1994). ISBN: 0395666112.

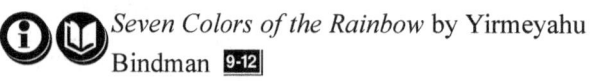

Seven Colors of the Rainbow by Yirmeyahu Bindman 9-12
Description: *Seven Colors of the Rainbow* is an easy read while providing a general overview of the history and laws of the covenant given to Noah and his descendants. After reading this book, readers can never again see the rainbow without remembering the seven laws. (Amazon reviewer). 138 pages (2000). Schueller House; ISBN: 0967620201. The first eight chapters are available online. http://www.schuellerhouse.com/scr_toc.htm

Internet Sources

ⓘ *The Flood Waters Subside*
Description: An excellent study, part of *Old Testament Bible Study: Creation to Abraham, Genesis 1 to Genesis 12*.
http://bible-truth.org/GEN8-9.HTM

ⓘ *The Spirit of the Law* by Dr. Ron Moseley
Description: Free book contents online.
http://www.haydid.org/spiritta.htm

ⓘ *The Universal Corruption of Man - Preparation for the Flood*
Description: Chapter 7 from *Bible History: Old Testament*, by Alfred Edersheim.
http://philologos.org/__eb-bhot/vol_I/ch05.htm

Step 3: Expand

Choose and complete one of the following activities:

Activity 1: Write a Diary Entry
Write a diary entry as if you were one of the people watching as Noah built the Ark. Did you think he was foolish? Younger students may dictate or narrate (tell back) what a person may have been thinking.

Activity 2: Write a Diary Entry
Write another entry as if you were one of Noah's children. Explain what you see, hear, and feel before boarding the Ark and after the Ark has landed. Do you feel opportunities to start afresh? Younger students may dictate or narrate (tell back) what a child of Noah may have been thinking.

Activity 3: Complete Worksheets
Complete the *God Sends a Great Flood* worksheets and puzzles.
http://www.calvarychapel.org/children/site/pdf/Old/Curr008.pdf

Activity 4: Create a Display
Draw a picture of the rainbow. Think of ROY G. BIV: Mr. BIV is not a person; rather, his name is an acronym for the colors in the rainbow: Red, Orange, Yellow, Green, Blue, Indigo, Violet. It is way to help you remember the seven main sections of the visible light portion of the spectrum (in order). Look for the colors referred to in *ROY G. BIV* the next time you see a rainbow. Add text to your illustration by pointing out that the Seven Noachide Laws parallel the seven colors of the rainbow.

Recommended in: ♦ several lessons in a unit; ★ several units in a volume; ● several volumes. ⚭ Key Resource for this unit.

Adam to Abraham

Activity 5: Draw an Illustration
The dove and the olive branch are important symbols. In Gen. 8:6–12, it was the dove that brought back the olive branch. Read Matt. 3:14–17 and Rom. 11:24. The dove and the branch are reflections of salvation that recur throughout the Bible. Draw an illustration of a dove and an olive branch. Share your drawing with someone, then add it to your Portfolio.

Step 4: Excel

- ❏ Correct all written work to demonstrate correct punctuation and spelling.
- ❏ Correct all written work to demonstrate correct and effective use of grammar.
- ❏ Add to your Writing Notebook the rules for all punctuation and grammar errors you corrected.
- ❏ Record any misspelled words in your Spelling Notebook.
- ❏ Add to your Vocabulary Notebook any new words encountered in this lesson. Include a definition for each word. Use each vocabulary term in a sentence orally or in writing.
- ❏ Add corrected written work or any illustrations to your Portfolio.
- ❏ Add any important people or events to your Time Line Book.
- ❏ Share with a friend or family member an activity you completed for this lesson. Explain to them what you have learned.

Footnote

1. Egne, David. 1991. Knowing God Through Genesis (The Discovery Series) [online]. Grand Rapids, MI 49555: RBC Ministries March 2001, Available from World Wide Web: <http://www.gospelcom.net/rbc/ds/sb111/sb111.html>
2. Moseley, Ron, The Spirit of the Law: Should Christians Reject God's Law? Edbed Publishing, Hagerstown, MD.

An Internet-Linked Unit Study

The Tower of Babel H10111

The Narrated Bible

Step 1: Excite

Imagine that you were one of Noah's children. The ark lands and you watch your father Noah build an altar to thank God. You hear Noah praising God, and you witness the miracle of the first rainbow. Do you think you would be full of appreciation that you were one of the few remaining people on earth? Do you think this would be an event that you would recount to your children to teach them about the mercy of God? Would you warn your children about the results of idolatry and sin? (Remember the Noachide laws from the previous lesson. The first law forbad the worship of idols.)

Ham was the son of Noah. One would assume that Ham would have taught his son Cush about God and God's commands. One would also assume that Cush would have taught his son Nimrod about God. But somewhere between these three generations the message of one true God was lost or changed, because Nimrod had no fear of God. Nimrod began a new pagan mythical religion and headed the building of the Tower of Babel.

Legend (not a Bible account) tells us that in the fourth generation, Nimrod's son Tammuz was worshiped as an infant god; he grew up and married the goddess of the harvest, Ishtar.

Ask your parents (and if possible your grandparents) about their upbringing. Are your parents first generation Christians? Did they receive Bible instruction? How has their childhood teaching, or lack of it, affected you or your beliefs today?

Step 2: Examine

According to Josephus (Jewish historian Flavius Josephus, 37 CE - circa 100 CE):

> Now it was Nimrod who excited them to such an affront and contempt of God. He was the grandson of Ham, the son of Noah, a bold man, and of great strength of hand. He persuaded them not to ascribe it to God, as if it was through his means they were happy, but to believe that it was their own courage which procured that happiness. He also gradually changed the government into tyranny, seeing no other way of turning men from the fear of God, but to bring them into a constant dependence on his power. He also said he would be revenged on God, if he should have a mind to drown the world again; for that he would build a tower too high for the waters to be able to reach! And that he would avenge himself on God for destroying their forefathers![1]

After the Flood, several city-states in Mesopotamia were united. These cities were conquered and established the world's first empire under Nimrod. His empire consisted of several cities or city-states, including Babel, which was at first one of a series of small cities, then grew in power. By 1700 B.C., it controlled an empire, known as Babylonian, which covered the southern part of Mesopotamia.. Assyria, or Shinar, was called the "land of Nimrod" (Mic. 5:6). (You'll find out more about the geography of

---

Recommended in: ♦ several lessons in a unit; ★ several units in a volume; ♥ several volumes. ☞ Key Resource for this unit.

Heart of Wisdom Publishing

ADAM 73

Adam to Abraham

these areas in the *Mesopotamia* Unit Study.) Nimrod brought together the people in various construction projects, including the Tower of Babel. Nimrod's identity is much disputed. He has been connected to the Mesopotamian god Ninurta, to the legendary Mesopotamian hero Gilgamesh (see *Gilgamesh Epic*), and to King Shamshi-Adad I, the founder of the Assyrian empire.

Nimrod was a son of Cush, grandson of Ham (who was on the Ark). Bible scholars refer to Nimrod as a "foreshadow of the Antichrist." *Nimrod* means "rebel" or "the valiant." He was a tyrant king, using religion as a political instrument. He led the Sumerians of Babylon to pay tribute to the sky gods (sun, moon, stars, planets) and convinced the people to sacrifice their children.

And Cush begat Nimrod: he began to be a mighty one in the earth. He was a mighty hunter before the LORD: wherefore it is said, Even as Nimrod the mighty hunter before the LORD. And the beginning of his kingdom was Babel, and Erech, and Accad, and Calneh, in the land of Shinar. Out of that land went forth Asshur, and builded Nineveh, and the city Rehoboth, and Calah: the same is a great city (Gen. 10:8–12). Most commentaries agree that the word *hunter* here probably refers to the hunting of men.

Amazingly, the people under Nimrod forgot God and His commands. The area was filled with idolatry. History records Nimrod and his wife contriving a new religion built around "the mother and child." This pagan worship spread throughout Babylon. After Nimrod died, his wife gave birth to a son, Tammuz, whom she declared was actually Nimrod reborn. This worship of a divine mother and god-child began long before the birth of Jesus. The mother-goddess appears under many different names: Isis in Egypt, Indrani in India, Cybele in Asia, Fortuna in Rome, Ceres in Greece, Shing Moo in China, Hertha in Germany, Sisa in Scandinavia, and the "queen of heaven" (Jer. 44:17–19). Among the Babylonians, Tammuz grows up and marries Ishtar, also seen as a goddess, who is portrayed as a mother with an infant child.

The people of Mesopotamia (present-day Iraq) built enormous step temples of mud brick called *ziggurats* to honor local gods and goddesses. The Tower of Babel was probably one such ziggurat.

An Internet-Linked Unit Study

Suggested Resources

If you would like to know more about the Tower of Babel, explore any of the resources listed below.

K-3	4-8	9-12
Read the story of the Tower of Babel in Gen. 11:1–9. If you are using the *Narrated Bible* ♥ Read page 17.		
Discovering Jesus in Genesis ♦ "The Tower of Confusion" (18-19).	*Discovering Jesus in Genesis* ♦ "The Tower of Confusion" (18-19).	*Discovering Jesus in Genesis* ♦ "The Tower of Confusion" (18-19).
Amazing Expedition Bible ♥ "The Tower of Babel" (29).	*Amazing Expedition Bible* ♥ "The Tower of Babel" (29).	*Bible History: Old Testament* ★ Chapter 8 "Genealogy of Nations - Babel - Confusion of Tongues.
God's Story ♥ "The Tower" (8).	*Adam and His Kin* ♦ Read: Chapter 15 "The Tower of Bel" and Chapter 16 "Aftermath."	*Adam and His Kin* ♦ Read: Chapter 15 "The Tower of Bel" and Chapter 16 "Aftermath."
	The Victor Journey Through the Bible ♥ "The Tower of Babel" (16-17).	*The Victor Journey Through the Bible* ♥ "The Tower of Babel" (16-17).
	Genesis: Finding Our Roots ♦ Read: Unit 5 "The Book of Shem."	*Genesis: Finding Our Roots* ♦ Read: Unit 5 "The Book of Shem."
	Nelson's Illustrated Encyclopedia of the Bible ♥⊙ "Cities, Towns and Villages" (120-121) "Buildings and Builders" (132-133).	*Nelson's Illustrated Encyclopedia of the Bible* ♥⊙ "Cities, Towns and Villages" (120-121) "Buildings and Builders" (132-133).
		The Bible Comes Alive Volume One, Creation to Abraham ♦ "Babylon: Where the Tower of Babel Was Located" (46-47).

Internet Sources

ⓘ *Is There Archaeological Evidence of the Tower of Babel?*
Description: Discussion of the reasons, methods, and culture surrounding the building of the Tower of Babel.
http://www.christiananswers.net/q-abr/abr-a021.html

Recommended in: ♦ several lessons in a unit; ★ several units in a volume; ♥ several volumes. ⊙ Key Resource for this unit.

Adam to Abraham

The Tower of Babel and Ancestry of Abraham
Description: An excellent study, part of "Old Testament Bible Study of the Creation to Abraham Genesis 1 to Genesis 12."
http://bible-truth.org/GEN11.HTM

Tower of Babel and the Confusion of Languages
Description: Offers a commentary illuminating the symbolic and religious meaning of the Tower of Babel.
http://www.ldolphin.org/babel.html

Ziggurat Challenge
Description: An online interaction game. As ruler of a Sumerian city, you have 180 workers to build a three-stage ziggurat. Your challenge is to divide the workers among different jobs. For example, if you have too many people making bricks but not enough people digging the clay, brick-making will stop. If you don't have enough workers laying bricks, the ziggurat will never be completed.
http://www.mesopotamia.co.uk/ziggurats/challenge/cha_set.html

Step 3: Expand

Choose and complete one of the following activities:

Activity 1: Write a Poem
Write a poem about the Tower of Babel. Refer to "Writing Poetry" in *Writers Inc*.

Activity 2: Complete Worksheets
Complete *The Tower of Babel* worksheets and puzzles. Memorize Prov. 16:18.
http://www.wesleyan.org/ssd/bkex/biblestorycards/BabelCard.htm
http://www.calvarychapel.org/children/site/pdf/Old/Curr010.pdf

Activity 3: Contrast and Compare
Genesis recounts that the two cities Shinar and Babel formed the original kingdom of Nimrod. The image of the city of Babel stood in sharp contrast to the nomadic life of Israel's patriarchs. The episode at Babel foreshadowed the dangers that Israel faced as it settled among the Canaanite cities with their rich temples and false gods. The main reason God punished His people with the exile in Assyria and Babylon was their persistent desire to accommodate themselves to the idolatry and lifestyles of the nations around them. Make a contrast-and-compare graphic showing how their actions compare with those of Christians today. Do we have difficulty living in a corrupt world? Why does God command separation? Visit the URL below for instructions.
http://homeschoolunitstudies.com/Ancienthistory/contrast.htm

Activity 4: Make a Display
Create a ziggurat out of Legos, sugar cubes, or other materials.

An Internet-Linked Unit Study

Step 4: Excel

Talk with your parents about sharing your faith with your children. How will you help your children remember God? Make a list of things you plan to do with your children to obey Deuteronomy chapter 6.

- ☐ Correct all written work to demonstrate correct punctuation and spelling.
- ☐ Correct all written work to demonstrate correct and effective use of grammar.
- ☐ Add to your Writing Notebook the rules for all punctuation and grammar errors you corrected.
- ☐ Record any misspelled words in your Spelling Notebook.
- ☐ Add to your Vocabulary Notebook any new words encountered in this lesson. Include a definition for each word. Use each vocabulary term in a sentence orally or in writing.
- ☐ Add corrected written work or any illustrations to your Portfolio.
- ☐ Add any important people or events to your Time Line Book.
- ☐ Share with a friend or family member an activity you completed for this lesson. Explain to them what you have learned.

Footnote
1. Josephus, Antiquities of the Jews, Book 1.4.2 <http://www.ccel.org/j/josephus/works/ant-1.htm>

Recommended in: ♦ several lessons in a unit; ★ several units in a volume; ● several volumes. ☛ Key Resource for this unit.

Adam to Abraham

Beginning of Nations H10112

Step 1: Excite

18–22
The Narrated Bible

Genealogy is a fascinating study and a wonderful vehicle for learning. Interview your parents, grandparents, and other family members about your family's ethnic background. What country did your family come from? How did they get to this country? What are some family traditions? Make a chart of three generations of your family. Free downloadable forms are available from the Internet at http://www.familytreemagazine.com/forms/download.html

Have you ever thought about all the different nations on earth? Do you remember the names of Noah's sons? Do you realize that all the people in the world come from these three men? The Bible explains how they were part of the origin of all the nations of the earth.

Now the sons of Noah who came out of the ark were Shem, Ham, and Japheth; and Ham was the father of Canaan. These three were the sons of Noah; and from these the whole earth was populated. (Gn 9:18, 19).

Step 2: Examine

After the waters of the Flood receded, Noah and his sons were told to replenish the earth (Gen. 9:1). All nations, all cultures, all tribes, and all peoples are descended from Noah through Shem, Ham, or Japheth. Anthropologists divide all the world's peoples into three races: Caucasian (white), Mongoloid (yellow), and Negroid (black). Within each of Noah's sons was the potential to produce all the variations that are evident within the three races of man. Gen 5:32: *And Noah was five hundred years old: and Noah begat Shem, Ham, and Japheth.*

> Shem: The line of Shem's seed was the covenant line from whom Abraham came, then the patriarchs, then David, and eventually Christ. *Semitic*, a word which refers to the Jewish race and peoples, comes from the name *Shem*.

> Ham: The peoples of Ham's line populated parts of Asia Minor, the Arabian Peninsula, and eventually the entire continent of Africa - once known as the "Land of Ham."

> Japheth: The Japhethite line goes to the non-Jewish (Gentile) nations. The Greek, Roman, and Egyptian peoples can trace their roots to the family of Japheth.

Some have interpreted Genesis chapter 9 to be the Scriptural basis for race discrimination. However, when God commanded Israel to be a "separated people," it was based on the principle of separation from sin. It is never based on what we determine as race; such as color of hair, skin, or eyes, or physical characteristics.

An Internet-Linked Unit Study

After the judgment of the Flood, the Book of Genesis records the the remarkable growth of the human community with its variety of racial, linguistic, and political divisions. Genesis chapter 10 is a summary of the genealogy of the three sons of Noah. It is usually called the Table of Nations. Noah's sons had seventy descendants (14 from Japheth, 30 from Ham, and 26 from Shem) the chart below is arranged into the fourteen categories to represent the tribes.

Noah													
Shem					Ham				Japheth				
Elam	Asshur	Arphax	Lud	Aram	Cush	Mizriam	Put	Canaan	Gomer	Magog	Madai	Javan	Tubal	Meschech	Tiras

Which Came First?

The order of the sons of Noah is not clear. Most commentaries believe Japheth was the firstborn. (Gen 10:21; 9:24) others disagree.

> *The Jewish Encyclopedia* says, "Japheth and his two brothers, Shem and Ham, were born...clearly indicated which of the three brothers was the eldest. Japheth usually comes third in order."
>
> *Harper's Bible Commentary* says, "The characteristic structure of the unit, in which Noah's sons are dealt with in reverse order of their significance, is also taken from Genesis 10 and becomes characteristic of Chronicles."
>
> *Smith's Bible Dictionary* lists Shem as the oldest.
>
> *Commentary Critical and Explanatory on the Whole Bible*: ...the account begins with the descendants of Japheth, and the line of Ham is given before that of Shem though he is expressly said to be the youngest or younger son of Noah; and Shem was the elder brother of Japheth (Ge 10:21),
>
> *Easton's Bible Dictionary*: Lists Japheth as one of the sons of Noah, mentioned last in order (Gen. 5:32; 6:10; 7:13), perhaps first by birth (10:21; comp. 9:24).

Seventy Nations

> This remarkable text sets Israel within the context of the world known to the Old Testament writers. It lists seventy nations (probably a symbolic round number; cf. the seventy sons of Jacob who went down to Egypt, 46:27), which represent all the peoples of the world, and is not an exhaustive list of all groups known in ancient Israel. It reads a bit like a family tree, but it may be that not all the relationships described are genealogical. In the ancient world, treaties and covenants led to people calling themselves brothers or sons of their treaty-partner. What the Table of Nations describes is the relationship between the different peoples, however they may have originated historically.[1]

Recommended in: ♦ several lessons in a unit; ★ several units in a volume; ● several volumes. ⊙— Key Resource for this unit.

Heart of Wisdom Publishing

Adam to Abraham

According to Jewish tradition tradition the seventy bulls sacrificed during the Feast of Tabernacles is to make atonement for the seventy nations. *The Wycliffe Bible Commentary* states, "Jewish commentators, following the Masoretic text, saw a correspondence of the seventy nations of Genesis 10 to the seventy Israelites of Gen 46:27."

In the New Testament, Jesus appoints seventy men to spread the Gospel to all nations. These seventy men may be associated with the seventy nations listed in Genesis 10.

> *After these things the Lord appointed other seventy also, and sent them two and two before his face into every city and place, whither he himself would come. Therefore said he unto them, "The harvest truly is great, but the labourers are few: pray ye therefore the Lord of the harvest, that he would send forth labourers into his harvest."* (Luke 10: 1-2)

It is important to observe that the three main divisions of peoples in the listing of nations (Gen. 10:32) are not always (or only) racial in origin. With respect to the sons of Ham, for example, we are told that they were separated out according to their families, according to their languages, in their lands and in their nations (10:20; see similarly 10:5, 31). *Families* is an ethnic term, *languages* is a linguistic term, *lands* is geographic, and *nations* is political. It is clear, therefore, that several criteria were used in describing the ancestry or location of this or that group of people. This may help to explain why a few of them, such as Sheba (10:7, 28) and Havilah (10:7, 29), are listed more than once. Perhaps, in one case, the division was based on ethnic or linguistic considerations, while in another case a geographic or political concern was most important. It is worth noting that skin color and other racial characteristics are totally absent from the Table of Nations.[8]

Suggested Resources

Learn more about beginning of nations by exploring any of the resources listed below.

K-3	4-8	9-12
Read the story of the Nations Beginnings in Gen. 10:1–31, 11:10-26. If you are using the *Narrated Bible* ♥ Read page 18-22		
Amazing Expedition Bible ♥ "The Nations Begin" (32-33).	*Amazing Expedition Bible* ♥ "The Nations Begin" (32-33).	*An Historical Survey of the Old Testament* ★ "The Dispersion of Nations" (68-71).
	Adam and His Kin ♦ Chapters 9 to 13.	*Adam and His Kin* ♦ Chapters 9 to 13.
	Genesis: Finding Our Roots ♦ Unit V "The Book of Shem." Focus on the "Table of Nations" beginning on page 80.	*Genesis: Finding Our Roots* ♦ Unit V "The Book of Shem." Focus on the "Table of Nations" beginning on page 80.
	The Holman Bible Atlas ♥ "The Table of Nations" (36).	*The Holman Bible Atlas* ♥ "The Table of Nations" (36).
		Bible History: Old Testament ★ Chapter 5 "The Population of the Pre-Flood World" and Chapter 8 "Genealogy of Nations"

An Internet-Linked Unit Study

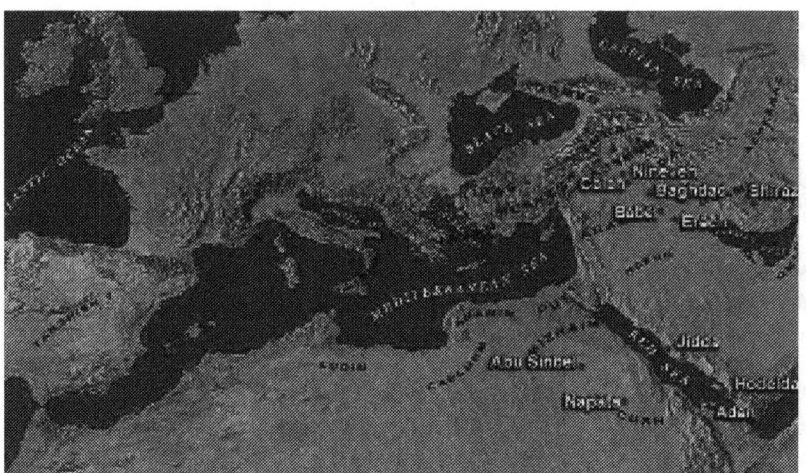

Table of Nations Map from Logos Deluxe Maps

Internet Sources

ⓘ *The Bronze Age before 2000 BC to 1000 BC.*
Description: MustardSeed Media time line that explains how long it takes for eight people to become twenty-five million.
http://www.mustardseed.net/timeline/timeline3.html

ⓘ *The Descendants of Noah*
Description: An excellent study, part of *Old Testament Bible Study: Creation to Abraham, Genesis 1 to Genesis 12.*
http://bible-truth.org/GEN10.HTM

ⓘ *Genealogy of the Believing Race, through Seth.*
Description: Chapter 4 from *Bible History: Old Testament*, by Alfred Edersheim.
http://philologos.org/__eb-bhot/vol_I/ch04.htm

ⓘ *Sons of Noah*
Description: Brief Bible study from "Daily Bible Study."
http://www.execulink.com/%7Ewblank/sonsnoah.htm

ⓘ *The Families of Man*
Description: Bible study on Gen. 9:18–28 by Ray C. Stedman.
http://www.pbc.org/dp/stedman/genesis/0330.html

ⓘ *Genealogy of Nations - Babel - Confusion of Tongues*
Description: Chapter 8 from *Bible History: Old Testament*, by Alfred Edersheim.
http://philologos.org/__eb-bhot/vol_I/ch08.htm

ⓘ *Shem*
Description: A dictionary entry from *Easton's Bible Dictionary.*
http://bible.crosswalk.com/Dictionaries/EastonsBibleDictionary/ebd.cgi?number=T3339

Recommended in: ♦ several lessons in a unit; ★ several units in a volume; ♥ several volumes. ⊙━ Key Resource for this unit.

Heart of Wisdom Publishing

Ham
Description: A dictionary entry from *Easton's Bible Dictionary*.
http://bible.crosswalk.com/Dictionaries/EastonsBibleDictionary/ebd.cgi?number=T1601

Japheth
Description: Another dictionary entry from *Easton's Bible Dictionary*.
http://bible.crosswalk.com/Dictionaries/EastonsBibleDictionary/ebd.cgi?number=T1970

The Population of the Pre-Flood World
Description: Chapter 5 from *Bible History: Old Testament*, by Alfred Edersheim.
http://bible-truth.org/GEN6.HTM

Table of Nations and Genealogy of Mankind
Description: An article on the descendants of Noah.
http://www.osterholm.info/man/

The Table of Nations: Genesis 10 and 11
Description: Bible study on Genesis chapters 10 and 11, and genealogical table of the descendants of Noah.
http://bible-truth.org/GEN10.HTM

Step 3: Expand

Choose and complete one of the following activities:

Activity 1: Review Maps
Today, the word *nation* is usually taken to mean a geographic boundary containing a large group of people under one government. This large group may or may not be related ethnically or tribally. In the Old Testament, however, *nation* usually had more to do with family, tribe, or lineage than with geographical boundaries. While these tribes lived in localized areas, they attached themselves to each other more by family than by area. Read Genesis chapter 10. Make a list of the different nations that came from Shem, Ham, and Japheth. Review the maps of the Old Testament, and locate where these "nations" lived.
http://www.bible.ca/maps/

Activity 2: Make a Family Tree
Make a family tree of Noah's sons. List their descendants according to Genesis chapters 10 and 11.

Activity 3: Answer Questions
Answer the following (see Genesis chapter 10 and 11):
1. Who were the three sons of Noah?
2. How many sons did Japheth have?
3. How many sons did Ham have?
4. Which of Ham's sons has the name of a modern country?
5. Who was the father of Nimrod?
6. Which nation will be a light unto the world? (Isaiah 42:6)

Activity 4: Learn a Hebrew Word
The Hebrew word for *nation* is *ywg* (phonetic - go'-ee). Add the word, and its phonetic spelling and meaning to your Hebrew Notebook (see *The Old Testament Hebrew Lexicon* at the URL below). The final words of Jesus' ministry, the Great Commission of Matt. 28:16–20, indicate how His ministry had expanded to *make disciples of all nations*. Use a Bible dictionary to look up and define the word *nations*.
http://bible.crosswalk.com/Lexicons/OldTestamentHebrew/

Activity 4: Trace a Map
Find a map in a Bible atlas or online showing the location s of the nations from the Table of Nations. Trace and label the map.

Step 4: Excel

- ❏ Correct all written work to demonstrate correct punctuation and spelling.
- ❏ Correct all written work to demonstrate correct and effective use of grammar.
- ❏ Add to your Writing Notebook the rules for all punctuation and grammar errors you corrected.
- ❏ Record any misspelled words in your Spelling Notebook.
- ❏ Add to your Vocabulary Notebook any new words encountered in this lesson. Include a definition for each word. Use each vocabulary term in a sentence orally or in writing.
- ❏ Add corrected written work or any illustrations to your Portfolio.
- ❏ Add any important people or events to your Time Line Book.
- ❏ Share with a friend or family member an activity you completed for this lesson. Explain to them what you have learned.

Footnotes
1. The Jewish Encyclopedia (NY: Funk and Wagnall, 1905), XII:588-9; The Universal Jewish Encyclopedia (NY:Universal Jewish Encyclopedia Co., 1942), 6:41.
2. Mays, J. L. 1996, c1988. Harper's Bible Commentary (1 Ch 1:5). Harper & Row: San Francisco.
3. Smith, William, Dr. "Smith's Bible Dictionary". 1901
4. Jamieson, R., Fausset, A. R., & Brown, D. 1997. A Commentary, Critical and Explanatory, on the Old and New Testaments. On spine: Critical and explanatory commentary. (Ge 9:27). Logos Research Systems, Inc.: Oak Harbor, WA.
5. Easton, M. 1996, c1897. Easton's Bible Dictionary. Logos Research Systems, Inc.: Oak Harbor, WA.
6. Carson, D. A. 1994. New Bible Commentary : 21st century edition. Inter-Varsity Press: Downers Grove, Ill.
7. Pfeiffer, C. F. 1962. The Wycliffe Bible commentary : Old Testament (Dt 32:7). Moody Press: Chicago.
8. Youngblood, R. F. 1997, c1995. Nelson's New Illustrated Bible dictionary Thomas Nelson: Nashville, TN.
9. Logos Deluxe Map Set, 1995 Review and Herald Publishing Association, Logos Research Systems, Inc.: Oak Harbor, WA

Recommended in: ♦ several lessons in a unit; ★ several units in a volume; ♥ several volumes. ☛ Key Resource for this unit.

Adam to Abraham

The Nations' Religions H10113

Step 1: Excite

The Narrated Bible

18–22

There are three major world religions that profess monotheism, or the belief in a single God: Judaism, Christianity, and Islam (A follower of Islam is called a Muslim or Islamic). Christianity is currently the largest religion in the world. It is followed by about 33% of all people—a percentage that has remained stable for decades. If current trends continue, Islam will become the most popular world religion sometime in the mid-21st century.[1] Over 69 percent of the Asian population and 29 percent of the African population are Muslims.[2] Saudi Arabia is considered to be 100 percent Muslim; Turkey is 98 percent Muslim; Syria is 90 percent Muslim and 10 percent Christian; Iraq is 97 percent Muslim.

Imagine that you had to live in one of these lands and interact with the people and shop at their shops. How would it affect you? How do you think you would feel living among so many people who believed so differently? Imagine and discuss the possibilities of moving into a town where the majority of people worshiped false gods. Missionaries deal with this they when they go to other countries.

According to *Microsoft Encarta Reference Library 2002*[2], the vast majority of Americans—84 percent—identify themselves as Christian. One-third of these self-identified Christians are unaffiliated with any church. See statistics from *Encarta* for United States religions below, left. The *1993 Universal Almanac* gives the Major World Religions below, right.

American Religions	
Protestant	55%
Catholic	28%
Non-Religious	8%
Other	6%
Jewish	2%

World Religions	
Christianity	32.4%
Islam	17%
Hinduism	13.5%
Buddhism	6.2%
Jewish	.04%

Step 2: Examine

After God confused the languages, men began to wander. So did their religions. From the beginning foundation of a belief in God, the various peoples began to change their religions to suit themselves. Similarities in the various worldwide stories about the Flood, Creation, and other things point to the truth of Creation and man's history. A primary difference between the truth of God and the tales that man began telling is obvious: Man's stories diminish or leave out God and give glory and credit to man himself. Thus, man began to worship the created rather than the Creator.

An Internet-Linked Unit Study

One of the most amazing inaccurate claims made today by unbelievers is that the Book of Genesis grew out of the pagan mythologies of nations like Babylon. Unbelievers have a theory that the stories in the Bible were taken from early civilizations, rather than the other way around. The truth is when God dispersed men, they took His teachings and perverted them into their own religions.

Each nation was dispersed from Babel, so they carried with them their memories of the stories of Adam, Eve, the serpent, the Fall, and the Flood. As time passed, man began to worship false gods. The polytheistic systems were formed in the Babylonian, Assyria, and Egypt continued to grow. Many of the pagan religions began as distorted stories. As the people started telling stories about many gods, they intertwined their stories with distorted versions of facts recorded in Genesis. The biblical account of the Flood is an example of this. People and tribes that have been separated for thousands of years still have a common belief that a deluge destroyed the world.

At the time when Abraham came to Canaan, there were a number of nations in the area. Each seemed to have its own god and religious practices. From Baal to Nebo to gods of Egyptian mythology, religions abounded. One thing remains the same; all religions, then and now, attempt to answer these questions: Who is God? Who is Adam (man)? What is sin? What is salvation? The difference between the true God of the Scriptures and these other religions is clear. All other religions try to reach God by works and by man's own strength. The Scriptures tell us differently.

Suggested Resources

If you would like to know more about the nations' religions after Babel, explore any of the resources listed below.

K-3	4-8	9-12
Amazing Expedition Bible ♥ Side bars (32-34)	*Amazing Expedition Bible* ♥ Side bars (32-34)	*Bible History: Old Testament* ★ Chapter 9 "The Nations and their Religion."
	Nelson's Illustrated Encyclopedia of the Bible ♥ ⚭ " Ancient Beliefs" (146-147). "Babylonian Religion and Beliefs" (64-65)	*Nelson's Illustrated Encyclopedia of the Bible* ♥ ⚭ " Ancient Beliefs" (146-147). "Babylonian Religion and Beliefs" (64-65)
	Adam and His Kin ♦ Chapter 17 "Gods and Goddesses."	*Adam and His Kin* ♦ Chapter 17 "Gods and Goddesses."
	Genesis: Finding Our Roots ♦ "The Religion of Sumer" (84) from Unit V "Book of Shem."	*Genesis: Finding Our Roots* ♦ "The Religion of Sumer" (84) from Unit V "Book of Shem."
	Our Father Abraham ♥ "The World of the Bible" (9-12).	*Our Father Abraham* ♥ "The World of the Bible" (9-12).

Recommended in: ♦ several lessons in a unit; ★ several units in a volume; ♥ several volumes. ⚭ Key Resource for this unit.

Heart of Wisdom Publishing

Adam to Abraham

Additional Books

Bible Lands (Eyewitness) by Jonathan Tubb, Alan Hills (Photographer) 9-12
Description: Photographs and text document life in biblical times, surveying the clothing, food, and civilizations of a wide variety of cultures, including the Israelites, Babylonians, Persians, and Romans. Hardcover: 64 pages, DK Publishing (2000); ISBN: 0679814574.

Islam, Christianity and Israel by Richard Booker 9-12
Description: In this small but informative booklet, Booker presents a clear overview of the origin and conflicts between the Arabs and the Jews and background, teachings and practices of Islam and how it differs from Christianity. Paperback. 34 page. ISBN: 0961530227.

Internet Sources

The Nations and their Religions
Description: Chapter 9 from *Bible History: Old Testament* by Alfred Edersheim.
http://philologos.org/__eb-bhot/vol_I/ch09.htm

Sumer: The Religion
Description: Brief overview of the Sumerians' worship of many gods, from *Mesopotamia: The Sumerians*.
http://www.wiu.edu/users/muems6/the_religion.html

Step 3: Expand

Choose and complete one of the following activities:

Activity 1: Contrast and Compare
God has said that He is the only God and there is no god besides Him. From your research make a contrast-and-compare graphic to compare Sumerians' worship of many gods with the Hebrews' beliefs. Then write an essay describing how these religions looked at God, Adam (mankind), Sin, and Salvation. Also describe how they looked at the life to come. Compare this with what you believe about the God of the Bible.
http://homeschoolunitstudies.com/Ancienthistory/contrast.htm

Activity 2: Contrast and Compare
Make a contrast-and-compare chart with modern day Judaism, Christianity, and Islam. Include: the history of how religion started, including key people and dates, major beliefs, religious rituals and customs, books, what happens after death, the meaning of life. Refer to the http://school.discovery.com/lessonplans/programs/islam/ and
http://homeschoolunitstudies.com/Ancienthistory/contrast.htm

Activity 2: Write an Essay
Write a paper titled "The Birth of Paganism." Refer to "Essay Writing" at
http://homeschoolunitstudies.com/writing.htm#essays

Activity 3: Make a List
Make a list of how modern-day America is like the Sumerian society.

Step 4: Excel

❏ Correct all written work to demonstrate correct punctuation and spelling.
❏ Correct all written work to demonstrate correct and effective use of grammar.
❏ Add to your Writing Notebook the rules for all punctuation and grammar errors you corrected.
❏ Record any misspelled words in your Spelling Notebook.
❏ Add to your Vocabulary Notebook any new words encountered in this lesson. Include a definition for each word. Use each vocabulary term in a sentence orally or in writing.
❏ Add corrected written work or any illustrations to your Portfolio.
❏ Add any important people or events to your Time Line Book.
❏ Share with a friend or family member an activity you completed for this lesson. Explain to them what you have learned

Footnotes
1. J.W. Wright, Editor, "The Universal Almanac, 1993", Andrews & McMeel, Kansas City.
2. Microsoft® Encarta® Reference Library 2002. © 1993-2001.

Adam to Abraham

The Call of Abram H10115

23–24

The Narrated Bible

This lesson will introduce you to Abram (God later changed Abram's name to Abraham). We will learn more about Abraham's life and family in the *Ancient Israel* Unit

Step 1: Excite

Imagine you are living very comfortable in a city, enjoying beautiful weather and a fine home. Your father owns a business and makes a good income. Then imagine God talks to you. He tells you to pack up all your belongings, your pets, and your brothers and sisters and leave the city you live in. You ask, "God where am I going?" and He answers "I'll show you when you get there. It will only take a few years." You will travel 500 miles away from all your family and friends on foot and will only stay in in a tent. Would you be obedient? Would you trust God to provide all your needs? Would you prefer staying where you are in comfort?

The Bible uses Abraham as an example of faith over and over. Faith plays a critical part in the life of anyone wanting to please God. Read Rom. 4:1-3, 16-24; Gal. 3:6-9. An very important part of faith is obedience. Abel was obedient, Enoch was obedient, and Noah was obedient. What part does faith play in your life? Are you obedient? Do you trust God with your future? Do you look to Him when making decision?

Are you related to Abraham? If you accept Christ as Lord of their life is adopted into Abraham's family! For all those who have accepted Christ, this lesson is more than a history study, it is a study of your family's history!

Step 2: Examine

After the Flood, eight generations after Shem (Noah's son) lived, Abram was born. As a descendent of Shem, Abram is a Shemite (Semite). During this time in history, Mesopotamia was the cradle of civilization. Abram lived a comfortable life in the city of Ur in a part of Mesopotamia known as southern Babylonian. Ur was on the main trading route between Mesopotamia and the Mediterranean. It is north of the Persian Gulf, in what is now Iraq. (You will learn much more about Mesopotamia in the next unit).

> Ur was an idolatrous city worshiping many different gods such as the god of fire, moon, sun and stars. Sin was the name of the chief idol deity of Ur. Ningal was the wife of the moon-god, Sin, and was worshiped as a mother god in many other cities. Ur was an evil and sinful city, as can be seen in the worship practices of the moon-goddess, Ningal. Every female in the city at some time in her life would have to take her turn in serving as a priestess prostitute in the temples.[1]

Most people believe Abram went from Ur to Canaan and stayed for a period in Haran. But he was in Haran long before he knew about God's plans for him. In fact, Abram was seventy-five years old when God called him away from his home in Haran. In Ur Abram was surrounded by pagans; his own father,

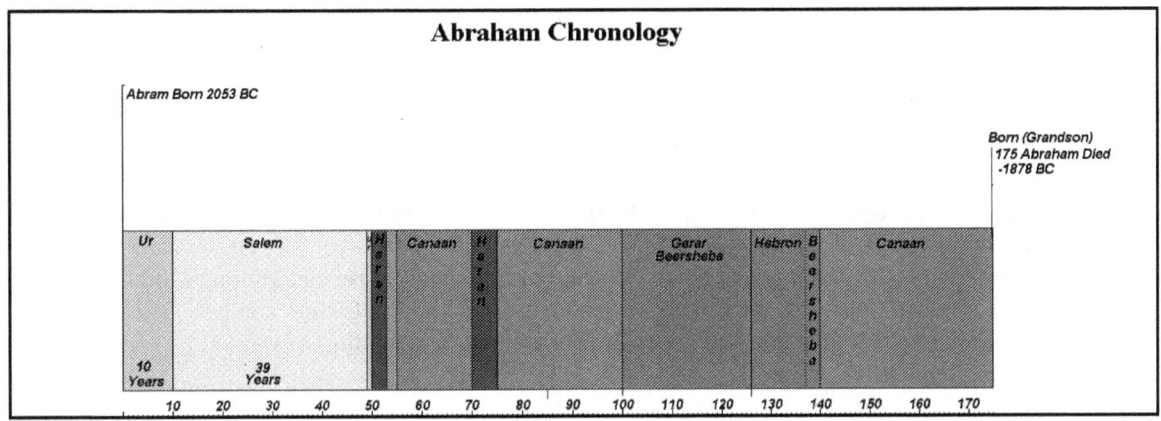

Terah, sold idols. Terah left Ur and took his family and household along the trade routes of the ancient world about 300 miles north and settled in the flourishing trade center of Haran, there they lived for fifteen years. While at Haran, Abram's father died (he was 205 years old). Abram was 75 years old, still in Haran when he received the call accompanied by a promise from God (Gen. 12:1-3). Abram took his nephew Lot with him on his journey, "not knowing whither he went" (Heb. 11:8). He completely trusted God to guide him.

> *Now the LORD had said unto Abram, Get thee out of thy country, and from thy kindred, and from thy father's house, unto a land that I will show thee: 2 And I will make of thee a great nation, and I will bless thee, and make thy name great; and thou shalt be a blessing: And I will bless them that bless thee, and curse him that curseth thee: and in thee shall all families of the earth be blessed.* (Gen. 12:1-3).

Abram responded by faith and obediently left everything in Ur and Haran for an unknown destination at God's direction. He traveled the 500 miles on foot from Ur to Canaan. The New Testament refers to Abraham's obedience by faith to his call from Ur as an outstanding example of faith in action (Heb. 11:8-19; Jas. 2:21).

Noah trusted God and built an Ark for the salvation of his household. Abraham trusted God and left his homeland for an unknown place of promise. Noah and Abraham were obedient and consistently responsive to God's Word. Noah's faith resulted in a 120-year commitment to the construction of a great ship despite public ridicule. Abram's faith gave him the power to leave all he had ever known to take an uncertain journey, not knowing where he was going. Both men trusted God and believed in a promise. God speaks and promises that in the future He will do something. This is the object of our faith, we trust God, that what He says will in fact happen.

Abram's call begins a new chapter in God's plan to redeem mankind. From Abram's family would descend people who would know how to teach and keep the ways of the Lord. God required obedience and personal commitment from Abram in order for this blessing to be bestowed.

What does Abram's obedience to God's call have to do with us today? God called Abraham out from the idolatry of his father's house (Gen. 12:1) and promised him an inheritance. This is a picture of salvation.

Adam to Abraham

1. We are called out of a sinful life to follow God.
2. God's grace is free—absolutely free. We don't do anything to earn it.
3. God must come to us before we come to Him.
4. God works a glorious work in our soul.
5. This call is not only to leave sin, but sinful company, and whatever else is inconsistent with our devotion to God.
6. God calls His people to an inheritance: by their response to His effectual call God makes them children, and so heirs of the promise.
7. This inheritance is not immediately possessed, but is something we can look forward to.
8. We need to fully submit to God's wisdom and will by faith. The faith to come to God is supplied by God. Implicit faith and obedience are due to God, and to Him only.

Suggested Resources

K-3	4-8	9-12
Read about the call of Abram in Genesis chapter 12; Heb. 11:8–19; Acts 7:2; and James. 2:21. If you are using the *Narrated Bible* ♥ Read page 23-25, 1652, 1626.		
God's Story "Abram's Travels Begin"(9-10)	*Adam and His Kin* ♦ Chapter 19 "Abram."	*Adam and His Kin* ♦ Chapter 19 "Abram."
Discovering Jesus in Genesis ♦ "God's Promise to Abraham" (20-21).	*Discovering Jesus in Genesis* ♦ "God's Promise to Abraham" (20-21).	*Discovering Jesus in Genesis* ♦ "God's Promise to Abraham" (20-21).
Amazing Expedition Bible ♥ "God's Promise" (33-35).	*Genesis: Finding Our Roots* ♦ Read: Unit VI "Book of Terah."	*Genesis: Finding Our Roots* ♦ Unit VI "Book of Terah."
Who's Who in the Bible ♥ "Abraham and His People" (8-9).	*Who's Who in the Bible* ♥ "Abraham and His People" (8-9).	*Who's Who in the Bible* ♥ "Abraham and His People" (8-9).
	Nelson's Illustrated Encyclopedia of the Bible ♥ ⚷ Review "The Patriarchs and Their World" (18-19).	*Nelson's Illustrated Encyclopedia of the Bible* ♥ ⚷ Review "The Patriarchs and Their World" (18-19).
	The Victor Journey Through the Bible ♥ "Abraham's Journeys" (18-19).	*The Victor Journey Through the Bible* ♥ "Abraham's Journeys" (18-19).
	The Holman Bible Atlas ♥ Read: "The World of the Patriarchs" (41-48).	*The Holman Bible Atlas* ♥ Read: "The World of the Patriarchs" (41-48).
		An Historical Survey of the Old Testament ★ Read: "The Founding Fathers" (73-84).
		Bible History: Old Testament ★ Chapter 11.

An Internet-Linked Unit Study

If you would like to know more about the calling of Abram, explore any of the resources listed below.
Additional Books

ⓘ *Abraham's Family: A Man of Faith* by John Morris K-3 4-8
Description: Do you know about Abraham, the ancestor of the people of Israel? His life is filled with mysterious adventures: the God of the Bible promised him land and an immense family! In this book you will read his story, which has been told for 4000 years. You will meet his son Isaac, a man who was faithful to God, his grandson Jacob, who struggled with God, and his great-grandson Joseph, the slave who became a prime-minister. You will thus learn how Abraham became the ancestor of the great family of believers to which you belong. Appropriate for ages 7-10. Softcover, 33 pages, Master Books (1998) ISBN: 0890512434.

ⓘ *Abraham: Called by God* by Witness Lee 9-12
Description: In a remarkable commentary on the life of Abraham from the Book of Genesis, Witness Lee presents Abraham as a genuine man, not unlike us all, fallen, but called by God. Like him, we have seen "the glory of God in the face of Jesus Christ" and have been attracted to follow Him. Like Him, we must learn the lessons of faith through trials, testing, and failure, in order to enter into the promises and blessings of God. Hardcover, 342 pages, Living Stream Ministry (1998) ISBN: 0736303596.

Internet Sources

ⓘ *Abraham's Faith Tested*
Description: A Bible study with questions to answer.
http://www.printedpage.org/lessons/lesson13.html

ⓘ *The Birth of a Nation (Abraham to Joseph)*
Description: Part 10 of "God's Story: From Creation to Eternity" from ChristianAnswers.net. (Follow the "next" buttons on the bottom of each page.)
http://www.christiananswers.net/godstory/nation1.html
http://christiananswers.net/

ⓘ *The Call of Abraham, Genesis 12:1–20*
Description: An excellent study, part of *Old Testament Bible Study: Creation to Abraham, Genesis 1 to Genesis 12*.
http://bible-truth.org/GEN12.HTM

ⓘ *The Chosen People*
Description: Brief overview of Abraham's relation to the Jews, from "Daily Bible Study."
http://www.execulink.com/%7Ewblank/chosen.htm

ⓘ *God Keeps His Promises*
Description: An article from Discovery Publishing, a ministry of Peninsula Bible Church.
http://www.pbc.org/dp/zeisler/4295.html

Recommended in: ♦ several lessons in a unit; ★ several units in a volume; ● several volumes. ⊙— Key Resource for this unit.

Heart of Wisdom Publishing

People of The Bible—Abraham
Description: Bible study by Charles Stanley from In Touch Ministries explaining that Abraham willingly obeyed God, not out of obligation but out of love.
http://www.intouch.org/myintouch/exploring/bible_says/people/abraham_156283.html

Those Who Have Faith Are the Sons of Abraham
Description: Excellent article describes how Jew or Gentile, rich or poor, male or female, white or black or brown, quick-witted or slow, old or young—anyone can be a child of Abraham. By John Piper, Pastor of Bethlehem Baptist Church.
http://www.soundofgrace.com/piper83/032083m.htm

Video

Abraham
Description: (from the back cover) "Emmy winner Joseph Sargent brings us the first in a series of magnificent Biblical epics from Turner Home Entertainment. *Abraham* is a powerful film, based on the most dramatic and moving tale from the Old Testament in which an ordinary shepherd is called upon by God to show his abiding faith in extraordinary ways." Available at some video rental stores. ASIN: 6303257828.

Step 3: Expand

Choose and complete one of the following activities:

Activity 1: Fill Out a Worksheet
Compile information from your research to fill out a Person Worksheet about Abram. Visit the URL below for instructions:
http://homeschoolunitstudies.com/Bible/Worksheets/people.htm

Activity 2: Make a List
Make a list of three promises God made to Abraham from Genesis 12:2-3 and Acts 7:3. Find confirmation of these promises in Genesis 13:14-18; 15:1-21; 17:6-8; 22:15-18; 26:1-5; 28:13-15.

Activity 3: Write a Précis
Write a précis about Abram (minimum 100 words). Refer to "Writing a Précis" (182) in *Writers Inc*. Share the précis with your family.

Activity 4: Trace a Map
Trace Abraham's journey on the blank map on the next page. Label the areas Abraham lived and traveled. Gen. 11:27–32; 15:7; and Neh. 9:7 describe Ur as the starting point of the migration westward to Palestine of the family of Abraham around 1900 B.C. Ur was one of the first village settlements founded by the so-called Ubaidian inhabitants of Sumer. A map of Abraham's migration can be found on the next page.

Activity 5: Examine & Memorize Scripture

Abraham's call involved separating himself from his country, his kinsmen, and his father's house. God was establishing an important principle: that His people were to separate themselves from all that hinders His purpose for their lives. *Wherefore come out from among them and be ye separate, saith the Lord, and touch not the unclean thing; and I will receive you* (1 Cor. 6:17–18). Separation is a continual requirement for God's people, from the corrupt world (Ex. 23:24; John 17:5, 16:2; 1 Tim. 3:1–5; Jas. 1:27, 4:4); and from those in the church in sin who don't repent (Matt. 18:15–17; 1 Cor. 5:9–11; 2 Thess. 3:6–15).

Pray and examine where you are in your life. Discuss these questions with your parents: Are you "separate" and out from among the world? Do you have friends who are unbelievers? Do you have friends in unrepented sin? The Bible firmly states that *bad company corrupts good morals*. What can seem to be innocent can result in great sin. What are the consequences of not separate? Read 2 Cor. 6:16 and Rom. 8:15–16. We must obey God's commands. Study and discuss each verse listed above. Memorize the two that speak to you most.

Activity 6: Write a Summary

Abraham possessed the faith that expressed itself in obedience. Write a summary of how Abraham's faith and obedience are a portrait of the saving faith we receive through God's Son. Younger students may dictate a description of Abraham's faith.

Activity 7: Complete Worksheets

Complete *The Call of Abram* worksheets and puzzles.
http://www.calvarychapel.org/children/site/pdf/Old/Curr011.pdf

Step 4: Excel

- ❏ Correct all written work to demonstrate correct punctuation and spelling.
- ❏ Correct all written work to demonstrate correct and effective use of grammar.
- ❏ Add to your Writing Notebook the rules for all punctuation and grammar errors you corrected.
- ❏ Record any misspelled words in your Spelling Notebook.
- ❏ Add to your Vocabulary Notebook any new words encountered in this lesson. Include a definition for each word. Use each vocabulary term in a sentence orally or in writing.
- ❏ Add corrected written work or any illustrations to your Portfolio.
- ❏ Add any important people or events to your Time Line Book.
- ❏ Share with a friend or family member an activity you completed for this lesson. Explain to them what you have learned.

Footnotes
1. Halley, Henry H, *Halley's Bible Handbook*, Zondervan Pub. House, Grand Rapids.

Adam to Abraham

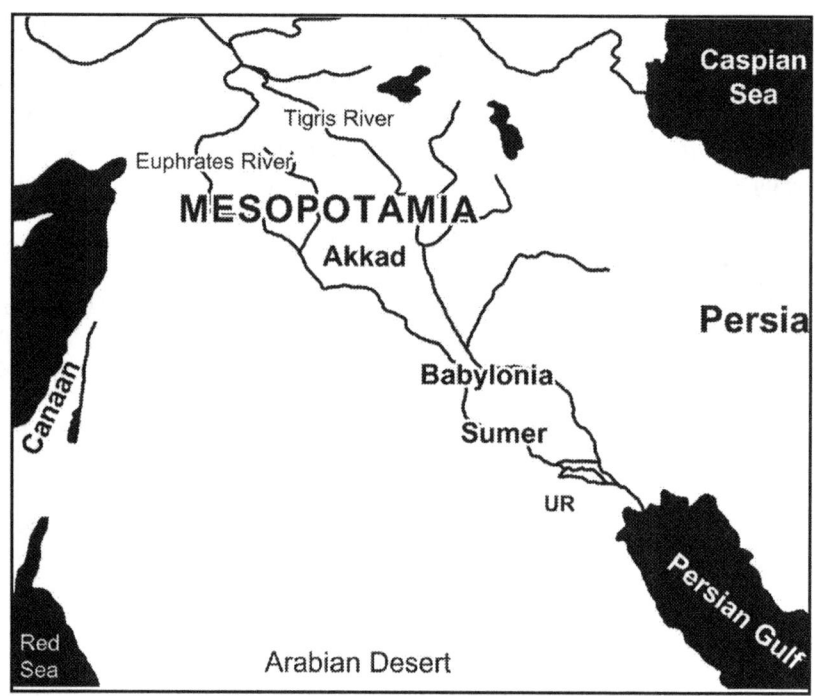

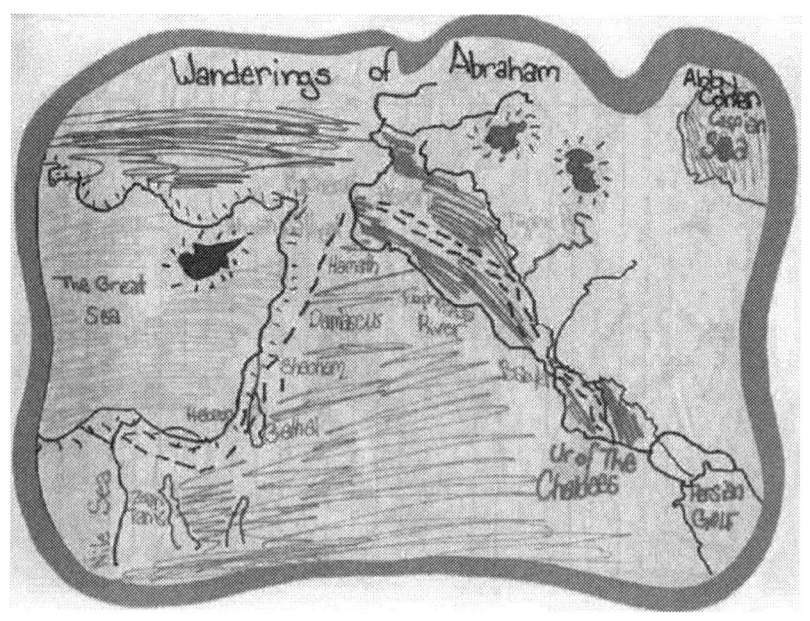

An Internet-Linked Unit Study

Abram Enters Canaan H10116

This lesson is about Abraham's first entry into the Promised Land. You will learn more about the Hebrews' entry into Canaan after the Exodus (Joshua chapters 1, 13, and 23) in the Ancient Israel Unit Study.

The Narrated Bible

Step 1: Excite

God unconditionally promised to Abraham and his descendants all the land of Canaan (Gen. 22:15-18). The land of Canaan (Israel, the Promised Land, and the Holy Land) is the most important place on earth. You need to know where it is and what countries surround it.

This land is the birthplace of the Judeo-Christian heritage. More blood has been shed for this land than for any other spot on earth. God Himself refers to Jerusalem, and to no other place on earth, as My City (Isa. 45:13) or more often, My Holy Mountain (Isa. 11:9; 56:7; 57:13; Eze. 20:40; Joel 2:1; 3:17). It is the place where God had His temple built and where He dwelt (Ps. 87:1-2). The Bible is a book about Israel. The Bible commands us to *pray for the peace of Jerusalem*. It is the place where Jesus Christ will come and establish Jerusalem as the capital of the whole world and rule over the whole earth (Isa. 11:9). If we understand God's purpose for the ancient nation of Israel, we can fully appreciate and understand God's redemptive plan for the world.

Few people today recognize how important the modern state of Israel is in God's plan. The Bible says that the sons and daughters of Israel would return to their land, the land of Israel, just before He would send them their Messiah. In 1948 Israel was re-established as a nation, after almost 2000 years of not having a national homeland. The Six Day War fought by Israel in 1967 returned Jerusalem to Jewish control for the first time in 1,897 years. Not a day goes by that Israel is not in our evening news. It is amazing that this little country in the Middle East, 70 miles wide and 300 miles long, has had so much attention.

Isaiah 27:6 says, Israel shall blossom and bud, and fill the face of the world with fruit. This prophecy is being fulfilled now. When Jews began resettling their historic homeland in the late 19th century the land was desolate, consisting of deserts and swamps. The Hebrews worked on turning barren lands into fertile fields. Israel today is a leading exporter of flowers!

In this lesson we ask you to make a map of Israel out of felt. You can use this map over and over for any Bible study for years to come. You should think of these maps as treasure maps! Because they will help you see real treasure—by opening your eyes to understanding the stories of the Bible. Maps give your brain a visual path through a story, helping you to understand the order of the events and visualize them. Once you get an understanding of where the events of the Bible took place, the stories will become more real to you.

Recommended in: ♦ several lessons in a unit; ★ several units in a volume; ● several volumes. ⊙— Key Resource for this unit.

Heart of Wisdom Publishing

Adam to Abraham

Step 2: Examine

How much do you recall about Noah's sons? In a strange way, the descendants of Noah were reunited when Abram came to Canaan. If you recall, Noah placed a curse on his grandson Canaan (Ham's son, Genesis 9:18-29) and a blessing upon his sons Shem and Japheth. Abraham, a descendant of Shem, comes to live in the land of Canaan inhabited by the Canaanites. *And he said, Cursed be Canaan; a servant of servants shall he be unto his brethren. And he said, Blessed be the LORD God of Shem; and Canaan shall be his servant. God shall enlargec Japheth, and he shall dwell in the tents of Shem; and Canaan shall be his servant.* (Ge 9:25-27).

Some call this land Palestine, but God calls it Israel. The name Palestine was a regional name that was imposed on the area by the Roman Emperor, Hadrian, who suppressed the Second Jewish Revolt in A.D. 135. He was so angry with the Jews that he wanted to humiliate them by emphasizing that the Jewish nation had lost its right to a homeland under Roman rule. The name Palaestina was originally an adjective derived from Philistia, the name of the arch-enemies of the Israelites 1000 years earlier.[1] Throughout the Word of God, this land is always called Israel, never Palestine.

Israel extends along the coast of the eastern Mediterranean. Lebanon lies to the north, and Egypt is to the south. The eastern border is the Jordan River. The pre-Israelite inhabitants were called Canaanites. We often think of Bible lands as desert images. But the land is described several times in the Torah as a good land and "a land flowing with milk and honey" (Ex. 3:8).

The Land of Milk and Honey refers to the fact that the land could support animals that provide milk and cheese, e.g. sheep, goats, camels, and eventually cattle, as well as flowering fruit trees that provided nectar for bees and fruit for jam. Animals and trees also meant there would be water. The promise of a Land of Milk and Honey confirmed God's blessing for the Israelites, considering the entire region is mostly arid desert. [2]

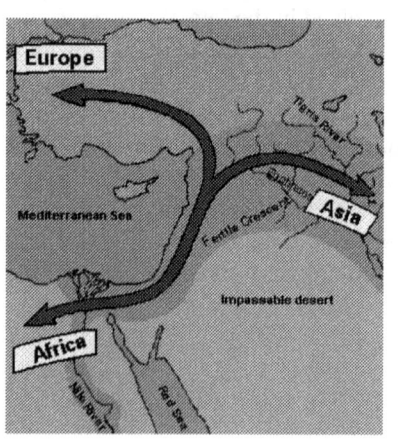

Canaan: An Important Land Bridge

Professor Howard Culbertson of the Southern Nazarene University discusses the important geographical location of Israel to spreading the Gospel.

Why did God ask Abraham to uproot his family and move all the way to Canaan? Missiologists have long pointed to the strategic importance of that narrow piece of real estate.

The Promised Land of Canaan is only 60 miles wide in places. At its western edge is the Mediterranean Sea. To the east is impassable desert. Its location thus makes it a land bridge between three continents. Africa's only land link to Europe and to Asia runs through what is today modern Israel. If God wanted to make Himself known throughout the ancient world, this would have been the ideal place to do it from.

To establish and maintain a nation on this busy bridge would be a superhuman feat. But this is exactly what the puny little nation of Israel did (with some brief gaps) for nearly 1,300 years. Was it a mere coincidence that God placed His people in the middle of this bridge? Unlikely. He seems to have done so on purpose so that His name would be proclaimed in "all nations."[3]

Suggested Resources

If you would like to know more about Abraham's first entry into Canaan or the land of Israel, explore any of the resources listed below.

K-3	4-8	9-12
Read about the call of Abram in Genesis Chapter 12 through 15. If you are using the *Narrated Bible* ♥ Read page 24-30.		
Discovering Jesus in Genesis ♦ "Cut Off" (22-23).	*Discovering Jesus in Genesis* ♦ "Cut Off" (22-23).	*Discovering Jesus in Genesis* ♦ "Cut Off" (22-23).
Amazing Expedition Bible ♥ "God's Promise" (33-35).	*The Victor Journey Through the Bible* ♥ "God's Covenant with Abraham" (21	*The Victor Journey Through the Bible* ♥ "God's Covenant with Abraham" (21
	Nelson's Illustrated Encyclopedia of the Bible ♥ " The Patriarchs and Their World" (18-19).	*Nelson's Illustrated Encyclopedia of the Bible* ♥ " The Patriarchs and Their World" (18-19).
	The Holman Bible Atlas ♥ See: "Abraham in Canaan" (47).	*The Holman Bible Atlas* ♥ See: "Abraham in Canaan" (47).
	Our Father Abraham: Jewish Roots of the Christian Faith ♥ Chapter 13 "Jews, Christians, and the Land."	*Our Father Abraham* ♥ "Jews, Christians and the Land (256-277)
		Bible History: Old Testament ★ Volume I: "The World Before the Flood, and The History of the Patriarchs."
		An Historical Survey of the Old Testament ★ Read: "Abraham: Genesis 11:26-25:8" (77-84).

Recommended in: ♦ several lessons in a unit; ★ several units in a volume; ♥ several volumes. ♥— Key Resource for this unit.

Israel

Adam to Abraham

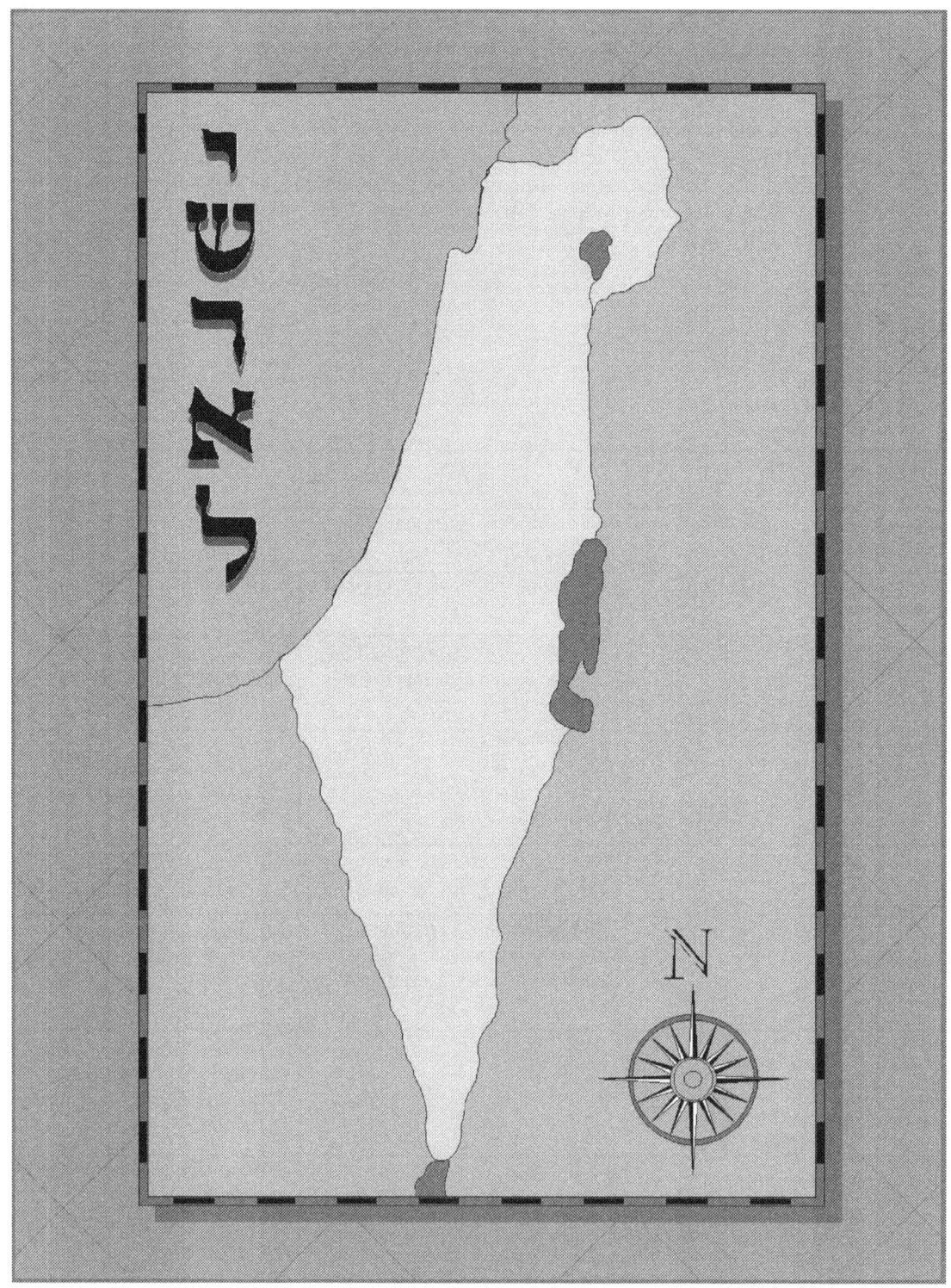

ADAM 98

Additional Books

The Promised Land by Linda Robinson Whited 4-8
Description: The Promised Land is a combination Bible story and activities book. The Bible story traces God's promise to give the people the land, beginning with the first promise to Abraham and ending when the Israelites enter Canaan under the leadership of Joshua. The story will help children ages nine through twelve make the connections among the various people in the Old Testament stories of the Hebrew people as they seek the Promised Land. Paperback, 48 pages, Abingdon Press (1999). ISBN: 0687081912.

365 Fascinating Facts About the Holy Land by Clarence M. Wagner 9-12
Description: Packed with a wealth of information about "Eretz Israel," the Land of Israel, *365 Fascinating Facts about the Holy Land* brings the region to life, especially for those who have never been there. From general information about climate, culture, and customs, to concise information about Middle East politics, wars, and efforts for peace, this book is the only handbook you need to understand this magnificent land. Paperback. 224 pages. New Leaf Press (2000) ISBN: 0892214899.

The Land of Many Names by Steve Maltz 9-12
Description: So much heat has been generated by the subject of Israel and Palestine. It's a subject that will not go away and it is crucial that Christians should have a clear grasp of both the spiritual and historical issues involved. This is a lively, entertaining and provocative introduction to the subject for ordinary Christians. The author takes you on a historical journey of the *Land of Many Names*, from the Canaan of Abraham to the Promised Land, by way of the Land of Milk and Honey, Israel and Judah, Judea and Samaria, Palestine, The Holy Land, Zion, Israel and The Zionist Entity. At each stage we pause to consider what God is saying to all concerned and, in some places, awkward questions are also asked of the reader. This is an easy read but it is not a comfortable book. Paperback. Authentic Lifestyle (2003), 175 pages. ISBN: 1860242871.

God's Plan for Israel: A Study of Romans 9-11 by Steven A. Kreloff 9-12
Description: This book will take you from the time God promised the land to Abram through Israel's history and into the future. This is a small, easy-to-read, much-needed book about a greatly misunderstood topic. *God's Plan for Israel* is an excellent, balanced book explaining God's mercy, grace, and faithfulness to the Jews and Gentiles. Kreloff, a saved Jew, shows how clearly the Scriptures distinguish between the church and Israel. Kreloff explains God's sovereignty in election does not negate human responsibility in salvation. Packed with much more than the study of Romans 9-11, this book combats the false doctrines claiming the church replaced Israel. Paul warns Gentiles (just as the Bible warns in Romans 11) not to "boast" or become "arrogant" against the olive root, which is the nation of Israel. Kreloff explains we must combat Gentile who consider themselves spiritually superior to Jews by focusing on God's grace. *God's Plan for Israel* is divided into three main sections 1. How God spared the Hebrew nation in the past 2. The reason He continues to preserve the Jewish people 3. The plan God has to restore Israel in the future. Paperback: 112 pages Loizeaux Brothers; (1995) ISBN: 0872134687.

Recommended in: ♦ several lessons in a unit; ★ several units in a volume; ● several volumes. ⌘ Key Resource for this unit.

Adam to Abraham

Internet Sources

12 Keys To Understanding Israel in the Bible
Description: Excellent article by Clarence H. Wagner Jr., explaining the *12 Keys To Understanding Israel In The Bible*.
http://www.bridgesforpeace.com/publications/teaching/Article-44.html

Ancient Canaan
Description: Site from William Penn Carter school explaining the culture, daily life geography and government of Canaan.
http://www.penncharter.com/Student/israel/index.html

A People is Born
Description: Heritage: Civilization and the Jews is a great PBS site on historical and present-day Judaism that features an interactive timeline, primary sources, lesson plans, teacher sources, images and more. These two sites include information and activities about Israel. http://www.pbs.org/wnet/heritage/episode1/
http://www.pbs.org/wnet/heritage/pdfs/episode1.pdf

Canaan
Description: Encyclopedia article from Britannica.com.
http://www.britannica.com/eb/article?eu=20200&tocid=0&query=canaan

Canaan: The Promised Land
Description: Article from BibleTutor.com.
http://www.lutherproductions.com/use30/level1/program/start/places/canaan.htm

Into the Land of Canaan
Description: Article from Antiquities Online. Includes a description of Canaan before the arrival of the Hebrews.
http://www.fsmitha.com/h1/ch04.htm

Step 3: Expand

Choose and complete one of the following activities:

Activity 1: Map Work
The best way to learn geographic locations is to draw them on maps. Copy the map of Israel from a Bible atlas or print one from our web site. Make multiple copies of a blank map of ancient Israel so you can practice locating the regional features several times. Don't let your maps get too crowded. You might want to put, for example, a certain type of physical features on one map and other types of cultural features on other maps. As you label cities and rivers, etc., try to keep your writing small so your map won't become over crowded. Names of areas (cities or water bodies) should be contained within those areas if possible. If not, use an arrow, or place a number in the area and put the name out in the margin of the map (like a footnote).
http://heartofwisdom.com/israelmap.htm

An Internet-Linked Unit Study

Activity 2: Make a Felt Map
You will need:
1. One large piece of dark colored felt (at least 8.5x11).
2. Velcro dots
3. Three or four of felt squares in red, yellow, and white (felt squares are usually sold by pieces 9 X 12 inches).
4. Scissors.
5. Hole punch (optional).

Use the map in this lesson as a pattern or print it out from our web site. If possible take it to a copy center and have it blown up two to four times the original size. Cut out the pattern of a large dark colored piece of felt.

As you complete lessons in the Ancient History units or during Bible study, make "markers" out of the smaller pieces of felt. Mark rivers and bodies of water with a fine-point felt-tip pin. Mark the names of cities on small pieces of felt. Use velcro dots to hold the felt pieces on to the felt (the felt will stick on but the velcro is much sturdier). As you learn about Israel, your markers can change to be the name of cities, events, or people. Keep your felt map and markers rolled up in a storage container close to your study area. Consider purchasing or making a flannel board to display your map. Flannel boards are available at various stores and at http://www.thefeltsource.com.
http://heartofwisdom.com/israelmap.htm

Activity 3 Complete a Map Study
Find Israel on a globe or in a map book. Answer the following questions:
   What is the highest elevation in the country (or the nearest country, if your finger landed on water)?
   What is the lowest elevation in the country (or the nearest country, if your finger landed on water)?
   Name an animal that lives there. Name a plant that grows there.
   How many square miles is it?
   What is the northern latitude?
   What is the southern latitude?
   What is the eastern longitude?
   What is the western longitude?
   What borders the northern side?
   What borders the southern side?
   What borders the eastern side?
   What borders the western side?
   Name a geographical feature within its borders (e.g., mountain range, valley, etc.).
   Approximately how many miles is it from the International Date Line?
   Approximately how many miles is it from the Equator?
   Is it north or south of the Tropic of Cancer?
   Is it north or south of the Tropic of Capricorn?

Recommended in: ♦ several lessons in a unit; ★ several units in a volume; ● several volumes. ☞ Key Resource for this unit.

Heart of Wisdom Publishing   ADAM 101

Activity 4: Contrast and Compare
Make a contrast-and-compare graphic to compare the first entry into Canaan by Abraham with the Hebrews entering Canaan under Joshua. Visit the URL below for instructions.
http://homeschoolunitstudies.com/TG/teacherhelps/contrast.htm

Activity 4: Make an Outline
Create an outline from the article *12 Keys To Understanding Israel In The Bible* at http://www.bridgesforpeace.com/publications/teaching/Article-44.html

Activity 5: Write an Essay
Write a traditional essay about the Canaanites, and include what they looked like, who and how they worshiped, marriage customs, approximate population, government, basic laws, their monetary system, entertainment, clothing, food, what their homes were like, their educational system and written language, the roles of men and women, their weapons and scientific achievements, transportation, agriculture, etc. Refer to "Structure of the Traditional Essay" and "Sample of a Traditional Essay" in *Writers Inc*, or "How to Write an Essay" (below).
http://www.riverdale.k12.or.us/~bblack/essayhow.htm

Step 4: Excel

Share with your family what you have learned about Abraham living in Canaan with the Canaanites. Discuss how the Canaanites' religion affected the other areas of their society. For example, how did their beliefs affect laws, government, and other aspects of their daily lives? Discuss how you think Christianity affects, or has affected, your society.

- ❏ Correct all written work to demonstrate correct punctuation and spelling.
- ❏ Correct all written work to demonstrate correct and effective use of grammar.
- ❏ Add to your Writing Notebook the rules for all punctuation and grammar errors you corrected.
- ❏ Record any misspelled words in your Spelling Notebook.
- ❏ Add to your Vocabulary Notebook any new words encountered in this lesson. Include a definition for each word. Use each vocabulary term in a sentence orally or in writing.
- ❏ Add corrected written work or any illustrations to your Portfolio.
- ❏ Add any important people or events to your Time Line Book.
- ❏ Share with a friend or family member an activity you completed for this lesson. Explain to them what you have learned

Footnotes

1. Wagner, Clarence H. Jr. *12 Keys To Understanding Israel In The Bible*.
2. IBID
3. Easton, Entry for "Canaan" online. Cited 2000.. Available from World Wide Web:
   <http://bible.crosswalk.com/Dictionaries/EastonsBibleDictionary/ebd.cgi?number=T703>
4. Southern Nazarene University, online. Cited 2000.. Available from World Wide Web: <http://home.snu.edu/~hculbert.fs>

An Internet-Linked Unit Study

Genesis Reveals the Messiah H10117

Step 1: Excite

The Bible is composed of 66 books written by many authors, over a period of many centuries yet it is one book, in its content, message, and theme. That theme is salvation through Jesus Christ. In the first book of the Bible, Genesis, God speaks Creation into existence. The heaven, earth, oceans, plants, birds and fish, animals, and humans are created by the spoken Word of God. Soon, corruption came into the world and enslaved man into sin.

The book of John parallels the first chapter of Genesis by opening with a portrayal of God speaking salvation into existence. *In the beginning was the Word, and the Word was with God, and the Word was God. The same was in the beginning with God. All things were made by him; and without him was not any thing made that was made.* (John 1:1-3). God's Word became human in the person of Jesus the Messiah. Jesus is the Last Adam (1 Cor. 15:45), and He came to earth to save the generations of Adam. He provides forgiveness for the broken and fallen. Jesus breaks the power of sin and sets the prisoner free.

During this Unit Study you have seen how the stories in Genesis chapters 1-11 (Adam, Abel, the Flood, Tower of Babel, call of Abram) point to Christ. In this lesson you will review the law of Bible interpretation that is best summed up in the following words by an unknown poet:

> The New is in the Old contained; the Old is in the New explained.
> The New is in the Old concealed, the Old is in the New revealed;
> The New is in the Old enfolded; the Old is in the New unfolded!

Open your Bible to Matthew 1:1-17. Have you previously read this section of Matthew? Or like most people, do you skim over the first 17 verses in Matthew and go to the story of Jesus' birth? Why do you think Matthew included this list of "begets"? How does this list of names relate to you?

Prophecies in Genesis about Christ:

- He would be born of the seed of a woman (3:15).
- He would be of the line of Seth (4:25).
- He would descend from Shem (9:27).
- He would be a descendant of Abraham (12:3).
- He would be a son of Isaac (21:12).
- He would be of Jacob, not Esau (25:23).
- He would be of the tribe of Judah (49:10).

Recommended in: ♦ several lessons in a unit; ★ several units in a volume; ● several volumes. ☛ Key Resource for this unit.

Heart of Wisdom Publishing

Adam to Abraham

My aunt recently came to my home for a visit. She has been studying genealogy for thirty years. I was fascinated to hear stories about many of my great, great, great ancestors. I doubt anyone outside of my family would find the stories very interesting. The stories were interesting to me because they "related" to me, they were about my relatives. I listened intently as she described where they lived, who they married, how many children they had, what kind of lives they lived, etc. The Bible is even more interesting when you understand you are a part of the story, part of the genealogy—the Bible is a story about your relatives.

Matthew shows Jesus is an descendant of Abraham. All those who believe in Christ for salvation are also descendants of Abraham. Jew or Gentile, Christians are *grafted in* (Romans 11 and Ephesians 2) or adopted (Galatians 3:6-9) into Abraham's family—Israel. Paul taught Abraham was justified before God solely on the basis of his faith, then explains how God saves all believers in the same way. Those who believe in Christ are the spiritual children of Abraham and the heirs of the promise.

> *Know ye therefore that they which are of faith, the same are the children of Abraham.* (Galatians 3:7)

As you review this unit, remember you are reading about your family. Because of Christ, you have a abiding position in the family of God based on the righteousness of Christ.

Step 2: Examine

In Jewish society genealogies were very important. A person's ancestry was his identity and status. Bible prophecy foretold that the Messiah would have to meet several requirements; one being the Messiah would be a descendant of Abraham. Matthew, a Jewish believer, begins his story of Jesus with the genealogy of Christ. The genealogy in Matthew proves that Jesus comes from the Covenant line. There are 16 references to the Old Testament in the first two chapters of Matthew. Matthew wanted to show the prophecies that the Jesus he described was indeed the Messiah Israel had been expecting. Jesus emerges from Israel and fulfills the promise of a Messianic King.

Matthew's book begins with the "genesis" of Jesus. The words in the Matthew chapter 1 "of the generation" is from Stong's number 1078, "genesis." The same expression is used in early chapters of Genesis (2:4; 5:1). Jesus the Messiah marks a new beginning.

> Matthew launches his Gospel with a genealogy, intended to serve as a record of origins of the one he will show is the promised Messiah of Israel (1:1–17). In summary fashion Matthew identifies key ancestors in the line of Jesus, with particular emphasis on His descent from King David. This is vital, for the Old Testament stresses the fact that the Messiah must come from David's line (vv. 6–17). At the same time Matthew wants us to understand that this descendant of David is more than a mere man. He is also the Son of God, conceived by a unique work of the Holy Spirit, in fulfillment of one of the most unusual of all Old Testament prophecies: A virgin will have a child to be given a name which means "God with us!" (vv. 18–25)[1].

There are hundreds of prophecies about Jesus in the Old Testament. Every detail of Jesus' life is spelled out in advance—from His birth in Bethlehem to His death on the cross. Review how Jesus is revealed in the first 12 chapters of Genesis by reading the text in the following chart.

Genesis Story	How the Story Reveals Christ
Creation	Genesis begins with the Creation story revealing Jesus *with God All things were made through Him* (John 1:1-3; 1 Cor. 8:6). God rested on the Sabbath—Jesus is Lord of the Sabbath (Luke 6:5)
Adam	Adam was given dominion over all on earth. (Gen. 1:26,28) Jesus was given dominion over all *in heaven and on earth.* (Matt. 28:18). *Far above all principality and might and dominion* (Eph. 1:21).
The Serpent	Adam and Eve were tempted by the serpent, Satan. Satan is our first enemy in the history of our salvation, he tempted Christ when He was praying and fasting in the desert. Jesus came into the world to conquer Satan and to free us from sin.
The Fall	Adam and Eve's sin corrupted mankind. God Himself made garments of animal skins to cover the sin and nakedness of His children (Gen 3:21). For the first time spilling innocent blood is needed for the penelty of sin. Jesus is the Last Adam (1 Cor. 15:21-22, 45). God sent Christ to be atonement for all sin. *For as by one man's disobedience many were made sinners, so by the obedience of one shall many be made righteous. Moreover the law entered, that the offense might abound. But where sin abounded, grace did much more abound: That as sin hath reigned unto death, even so might grace reign through righteousness unto eternal life by Jesus Christ our Lord.* (Romans 5:19-6:1). Sin and death are destroyed by Christ (Rom. 6:6-9, 1 Cor. 15:26).
Cain and Abel	Abel the shepherd brings a blood offering (possibly a lamb) that was accepted by God. Jesus Christ is the Lamb of God which taketh away the sin of the world.(John 1:29; Isa. 53:7; Matt. 26:53, 54; Luke 23:9). In contrast Cain offered fruit of his own work. (Hebrews 11:4). God illustrates the awesome power of the sacrificed lamb. One lamb saves a man, then a household, then a nation, and finally is available through the Lamb of God for the whole world.
Noah and the Flood	The story of the Flood is a picture of salvation by grace. That Noah's work brings blessing to all creation is seen from the fact that the animals and birds were also preserved in the Ark. *And God remembered Noah, and every living thing, and all the cattle that was with him in the ark* (Genesis 8:1). So, too, the work of Christ shall yet bring blessing to the beasts of the field. At His return to the earth *the creation itself also shall be delivered from the bondage of corruption into the glorious liberty of the children of God* (Rom. 8:21).
Tower of Babel	Man's pride and arrogance were revealed in the story of the Tower of Babel. God confused their languages; they were not able to understand each other, then he dispersed them around the world. During Pentecost, all understood each other with the language of love through Christ.
Call of Abram	Abram believed God. He left everything and went out of his country without knowing where, *"God will provide"* (Ro.4:16, Ge.22:8). God promised Abraham, the Messiah will be born of his descendants, that all the nations will be blessed through him. This promise was be repeated three times and it was fulfilled in Mat.1:1.

Recommended in: ♦ several lessons in a unit; ★ several units in a volume; ♥ several volumes. ☚— Key Resource for this unit.

Suggested Resources

If you would like to know more about how Genesis or the Old Testament tells us about Jesus, explore any of the resources listed below.

Knowing God Through the Old Testament by David Egner 9-12
Description: Each book of the Bible reveals God's character to us in a unique way. As we look at Genesis, the book of beginnings, it stands to reason that we will discover vital information about God's nature and character. And first impressions are often the most accurate. This book will help you to know God more intimately by giving you glimpses of Him as first revealed in Genesis. Portions of the Introduction of valuable little book are available online free. A Discovery Series Booklet from Radio Bible Class from (616) 974-2210.

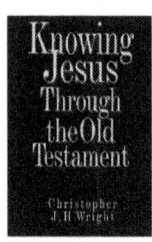

Knowing Jesus Through the Old Testament by Christopher Wright 9-12
Description: Has the Bible bound believers to a narrow and mistaken notion of Jesus? Should we listen to other gospels, other sayings of Jesus, that claim to enlarge and correct a mistaken story of Jesus? Is the real Jesus entangled in a web of the church's version of Scripture, awaiting liberation from our childhood faith so He might speak to our pluralistic world? To start to answer these questions we need to know what story Jesus claimed for himself. Christopher Wright is convinced that Jesus' own story is rooted in the story of Israel. Throughout His life Jesus lived by the Scriptures of Israel. Only as we come to understand Jesus as a man with a story—an Old Testament story—will we come to know who Jesus really is. To change that narrative is to deface our only reliable portrait of Jesus. Here is a book that traces out the face of Christ in the textual tapestry of the Old Testament; but it also outlines the pattern of God's design for Israel as it is lived out in the story of Jesus. Paperback, 276 pages, Inter-varsity Press (1995). ISBN: 0830816933.

Portraits of Christ in Genesis by Martin R. DeHaan 9-12
Description: Christian readers of all levels will enjoy this scholarly examination of how the lives of Adam, Abel, Isaac, Joseph, and other figures from Genesis were prophetic of the life and ministry of Jesus. Originally a series of radio messages, these studies were edited for publication by Dr. DeHaan shortly before his death. Paperback, 192 pages, Kregel (1995) ISBN: 0825424763.

The Messiah in the Old Testament by Walter C. Kaiser Jr. 9-12
Description: Old Testament texts that point to the coming of the Messiah are traditionally interpreted either from the viewpoint of their New Testament fulfillment (evangelicalism) or their linguistic and grammatical distinctiveness within the Hebrew Bible (non-conservative). *The Messiah in the Old Testament* considers another important line of interpretation that has been neglected in building an Old Testament theology. It approaches Israel's concept of the Messiah as a developing theme and shows how a proper grasp of the textual meaning at each stage of Old Testament revelation is necessary for understanding Messianic prophecy. Beginning in the Pentateuch and working through the Old Testament to the Minor Prophets, the author delineates texts that are direct Messianic prophecies and examines their meaning and development within the flow of God's plan. The reader will gain an understanding of God's process

for bringing the Messiah to earth through the nation of Israel, and of his intent to bring the saving knowledge of Christ to the world through them. Paperback, 256 pages, Zondervan (1995). ISBN: 031020030X.

The Unfolding Mystery: Discovering Christ in the Old Testament by Edmund P. Clowney 9-12
Description: Beginning with Adam and Eve and continuing through to the last of the Prophets, Dr. Clowney takes a fascinating walk through the Old Testament, revealing Christ in places where He is usually overlooked. Paperback, 202 pages, P&R Publishing (1988). ISBN: 0875521746.

Internet Sources

Does the New Testament Support Genesis 1–11?
Description: The early chapters of Genesis were frequently referred to by every New Testament writer and by Jesus Christ Himself. This site lists sixty-eight direct references in the New Testament that refer back to these foundational chapters of Genesis. (Based in part on the original work of Dr. Henry M. Morris as contained in his book, *The Remarkable Birth of Planet Earth*.)
http://www.creationscience.com/onlinebook/FAQ43.html

Fulfilled Messianic Prophecies from Genesis
Description: Several tables with prophecy, fulfillment, and commentary.
http://www.messiahrevealed.org/genesis.html

Jesus Christ in Genesis
Description: Article from "Knowing God Through Genesis."
http://www.gospelcom.net/rbc/ds/sb111/page5.html

The Messiah In Prophecy
Description: This study explains how, over twenty Old Testament writers over a span of some two thousand years portray the picture of a coming Messiah.
http://www.westarkchurchofchrist.org/wings/lbcprophecy.htm

The Two Trees: A Picture of Grace
Description: Bible study from a Baptist church
http://www.freegrace.net/articles/web/Don_Fortner25.htm

The Two Adams and the Two Trees
Description: Bible study from *Let Us Reason*.
http://www.letusreason.org/Doct7.htm

The Revelation of Jesus Christ in Genesis
Description: Bible study from a BibleBooks.com
http://www.biblebooks.com/Bibleclass/relevation.html

Recommended in: ♦ several lessons in a unit; ★ several units in a volume; ● several volumes. ☛ Key Resource for this unit.

Heart of Wisdom Publishing

Adam to Abraham

Step 3: Expand

Complete one or more of the following activities:

Activity 1: Match the Story
Match the Bible stories in Genesis with the appropriate text revealing Jesus. Look up the Bible verses for hints. The first one is done for you.

Bible Story	Genesis
1. Creation: God spoke Creation into existence.	1:1
2. Adam: First man, given dominion over Creation	1:28
3. Eve: First woman, first in the transgression.	3:15
4. Satan: An angel from heaven fell from pride.	
5. The Fall: Corrupted man and placed all mankind into the bondage of sin.	3:1-21
6. Cain and Abel: God accepts the blood sacrifice as temporary atonement for sin.	4:8-10
7. Flood and Rainbow: Salvation from judgement and a promise.	9:13-15
8. Tower of Babel: Man without God equals confusion.	11:9
9. Promises to Abraham: All the nations will be blessed through him.	22:15-19

How Christ Fulfilled	Verses
a. Jesus came to offer salvation from judgment.	John 3:16
b. Through Christ there is unity.	Acts 2:11
c. When we believe in Christ we are adopted into His family and become heirs with Him.	Gal 3,
d. Christ came to redeem and set the prisoners free.	GAl 3:13
d. Jesus Christ's blood takes away the sin of the world. (John 1:29; Isa. 53:7; Matt. 26:53, 54; Luke 23:9).	Luke 22:20; Heb 9:22; 12:24,
e. Christ is ruler over heaven and earth.	Romans 5:14; 1Co 15:45
f. Christ was present and active when this was spoken into existence. Christ is the Word in human form.	John 1:1
g. God's grace is magnified as the promise of salvation is from the seed of this one.	Luke 3
h. Jesus came into the world to conquer him.	1John 3:8

1 → f

Activity 2: Make a Chart
Create a visual chart. Make either a *Types of Christ from Genesis* chart or a *Prophecies of Christ in Genesis* chart. Include columns showing the similarities and Bible references.

Activity 3: Make a Chart
Jesus taught from the only Bible He had—the Old Testament. Make a chart with two columns. List what Jesus taught about each of the following people:
- Abel (Luke 11:51)
- Noah (Matt. 24:37-39)
- Abraham (John 8:56)
- Lot (Luke 17:28-32) Elijah (Luke 4:25)
- Elisha (Luke 4:27)
- Jonah (Matt. 12:9-41)

Activity 4: Create an Outline
Outline Genesis chapters 1-11 showing typical pictures and prophetic foreshadowings of Jesus Christ.

Activity 5: Create an Outline
Outline the book *Discovering Jesus in Genesis* showing typical pictures and prophetic foreshadowings of Jesus Christ.

Step 4: Excel

- ☐ Correct all written work to demonstrate correct punctuation and spelling.
- ☐ Correct all written work to demonstrate correct and effective use of grammar.
- ☐ Add to your Writing Notebook the rules for all punctuation and grammar errors you corrected.
- ☐ Record any misspelled words in your Spelling Notebook.
- ☐ Add to your Vocabulary Notebook any new words encountered in this lesson. Include a definition for each word. Use each vocabulary term in a sentence orally or in writing.
- ☐ Add corrected written work or any illustrations to your Portfolio.
- ☐ Add any important people or events to your Time Line Book.
- ☐ Share with a friend or family member an activity you completed for this lesson. Explain to them what you have learned

Footnotes
1. Richards, L. 1991. *The Bible Reader's Companion.* (Mt 1:1). Victor Books: Wheaton, Ill.
2. Keathley, J. Hampton III. 1998. *Concise Old Testament Survey, Biblical Studies Foundation* [online]. [Cited April 2000.] Available from World Wide Web: <http://www.bible.org/docs/out/survey/toc.htm>
3. Egner, David. 1991. Knowing God Through Genesis, RBC Ministries [online]. <http://www.gospelcom.net/rbc/ds/sb111/>

Recommended in: ♦ several lessons in a unit; ★ several units in a volume; ● several volumes. ⊙— Key Resource for this unit.

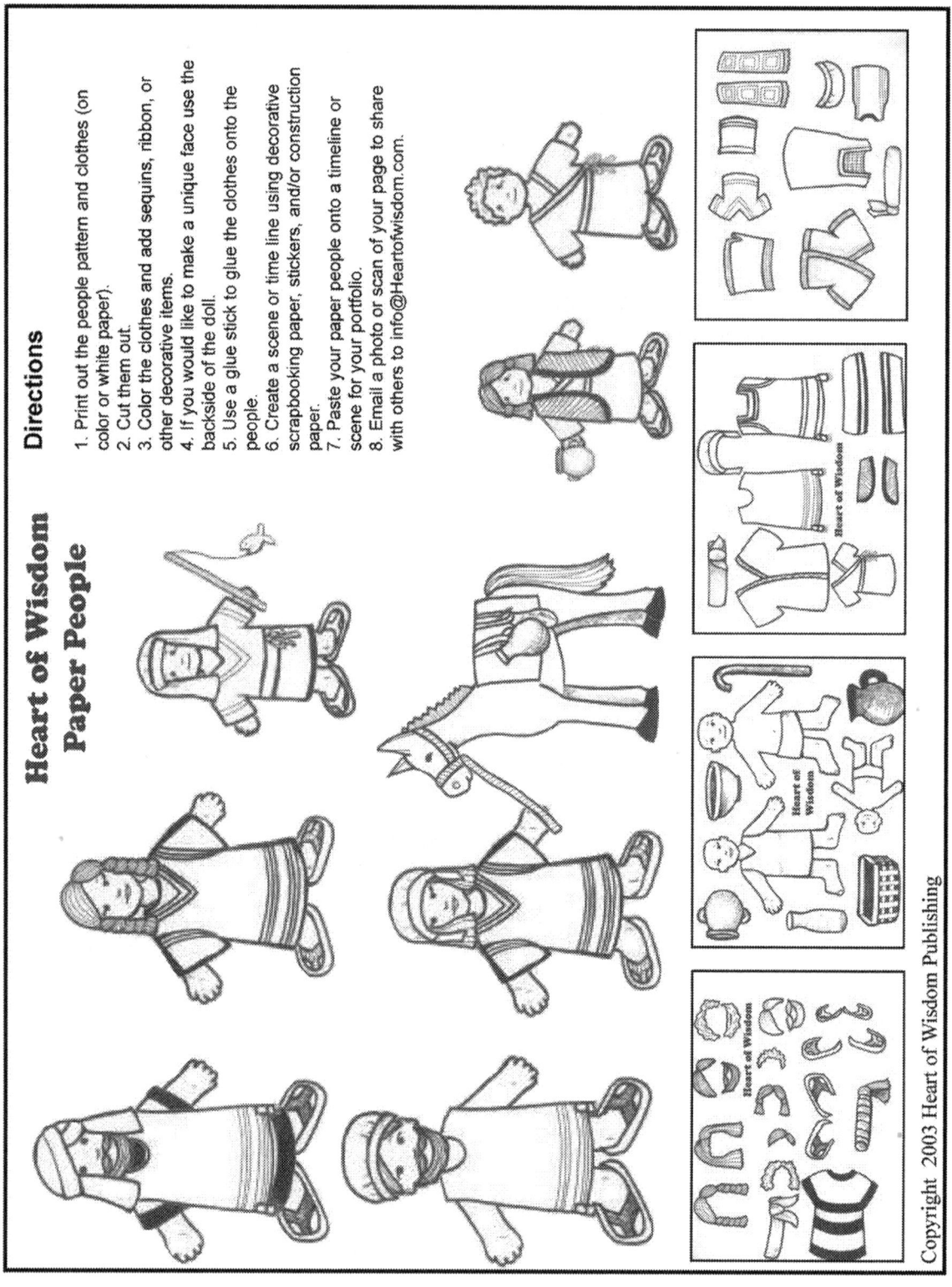

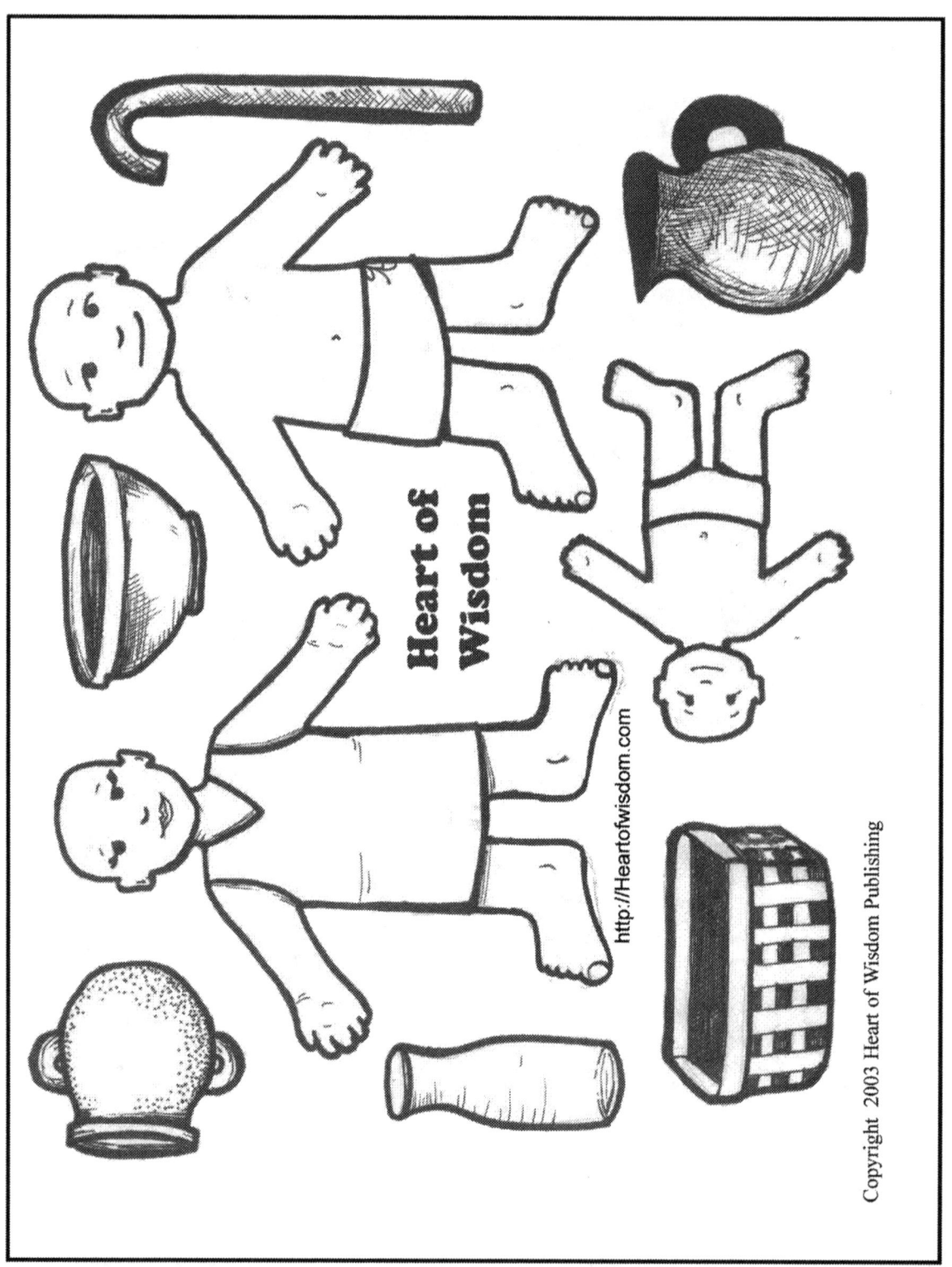

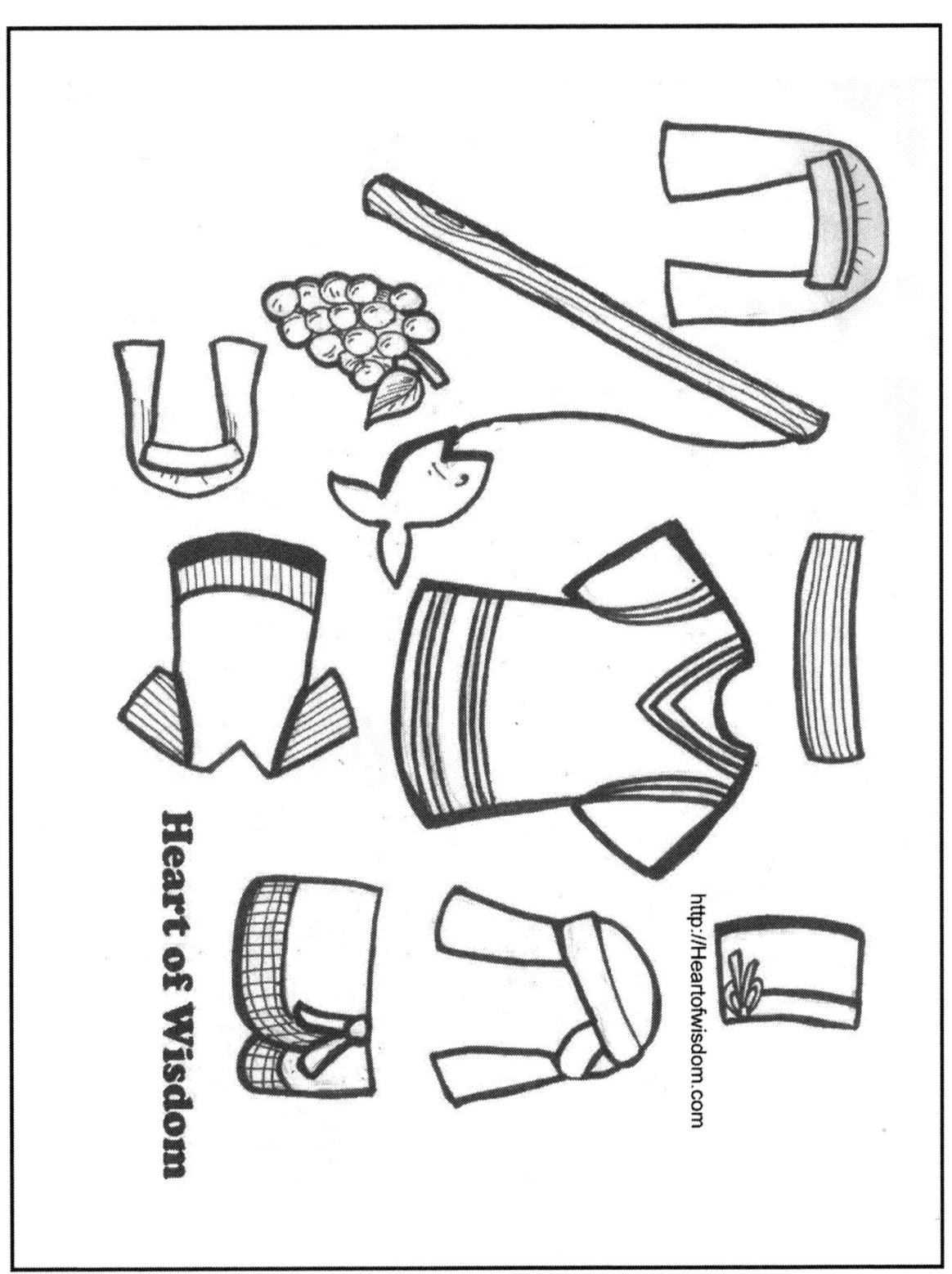

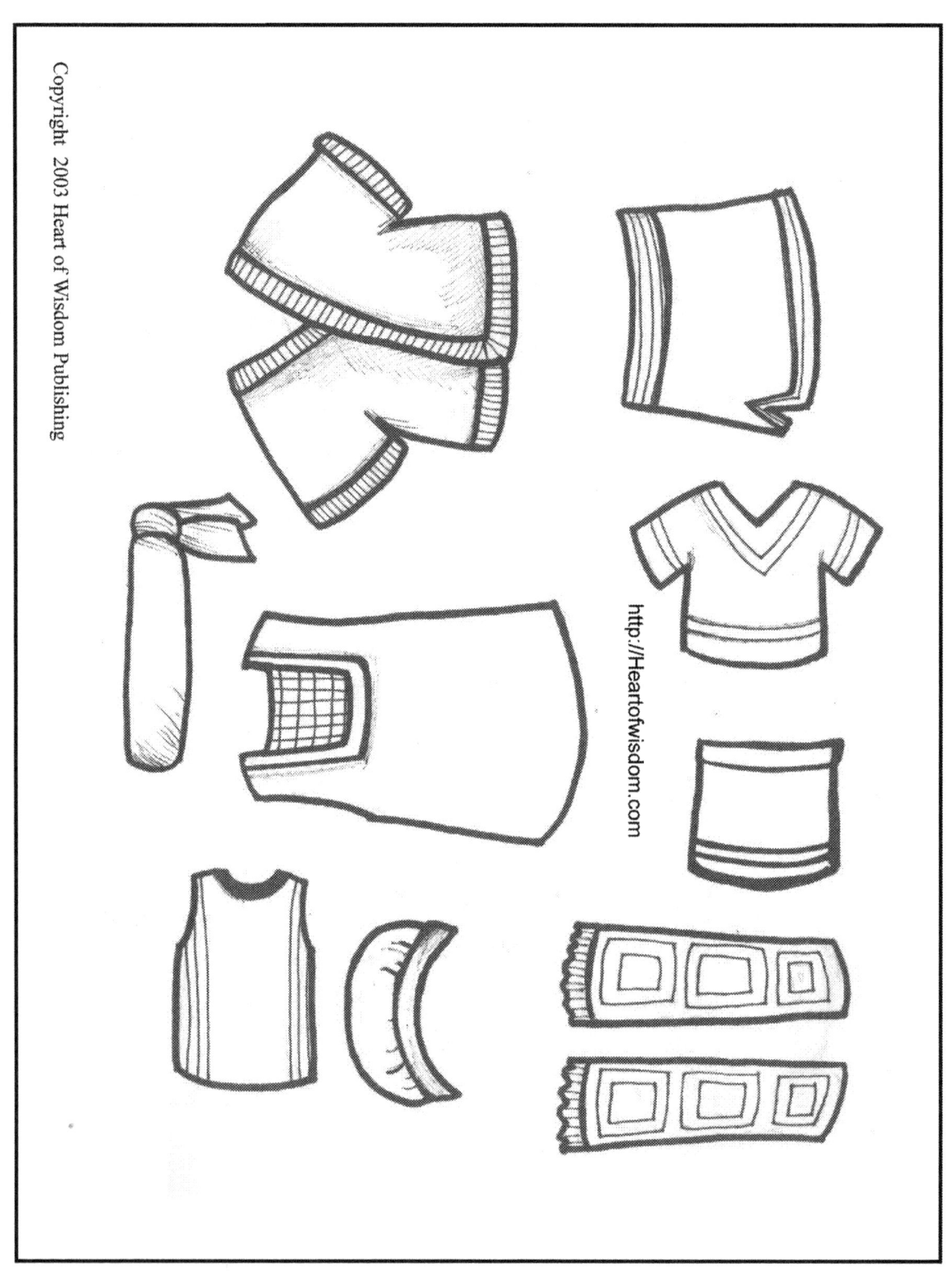

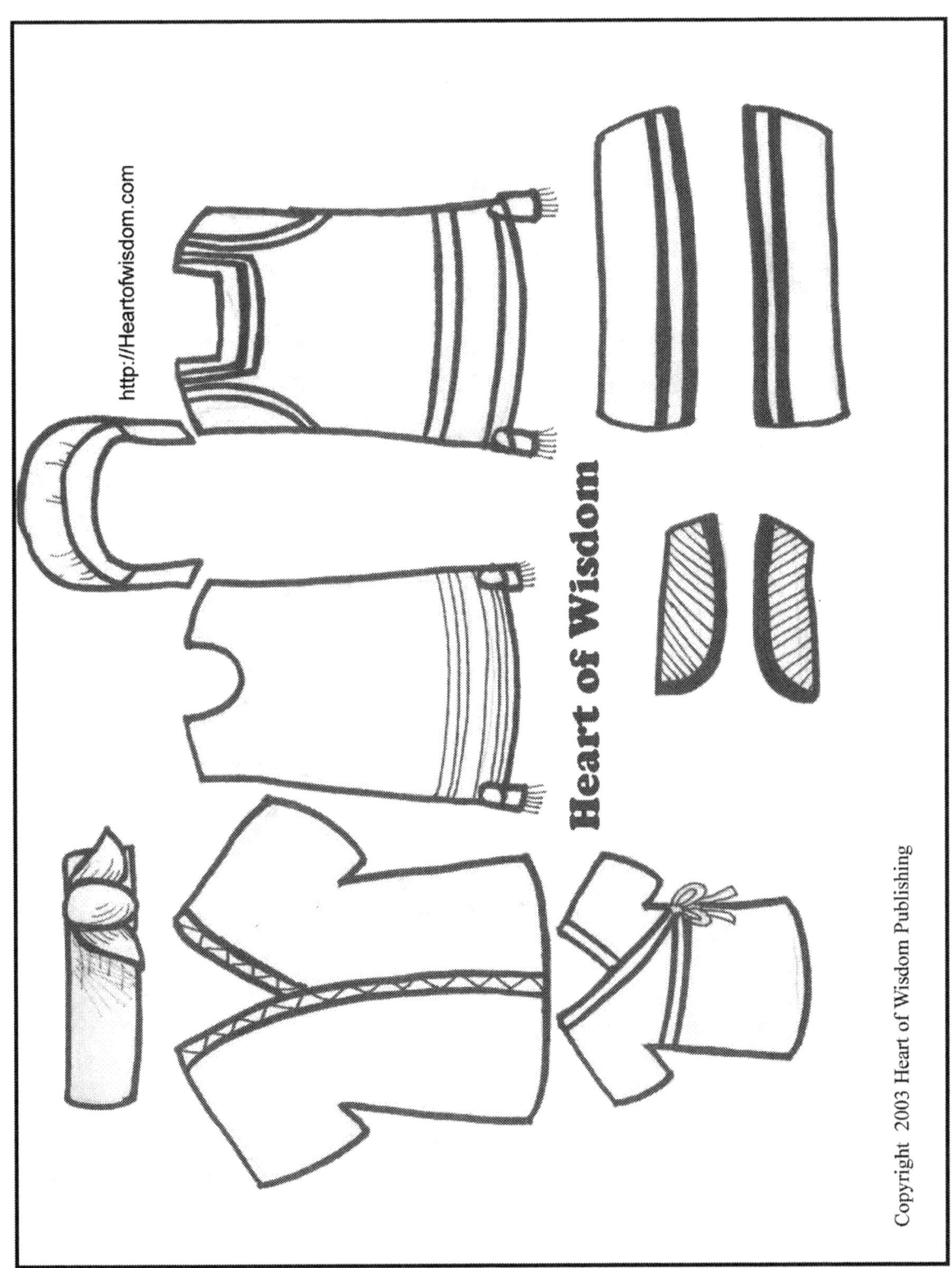

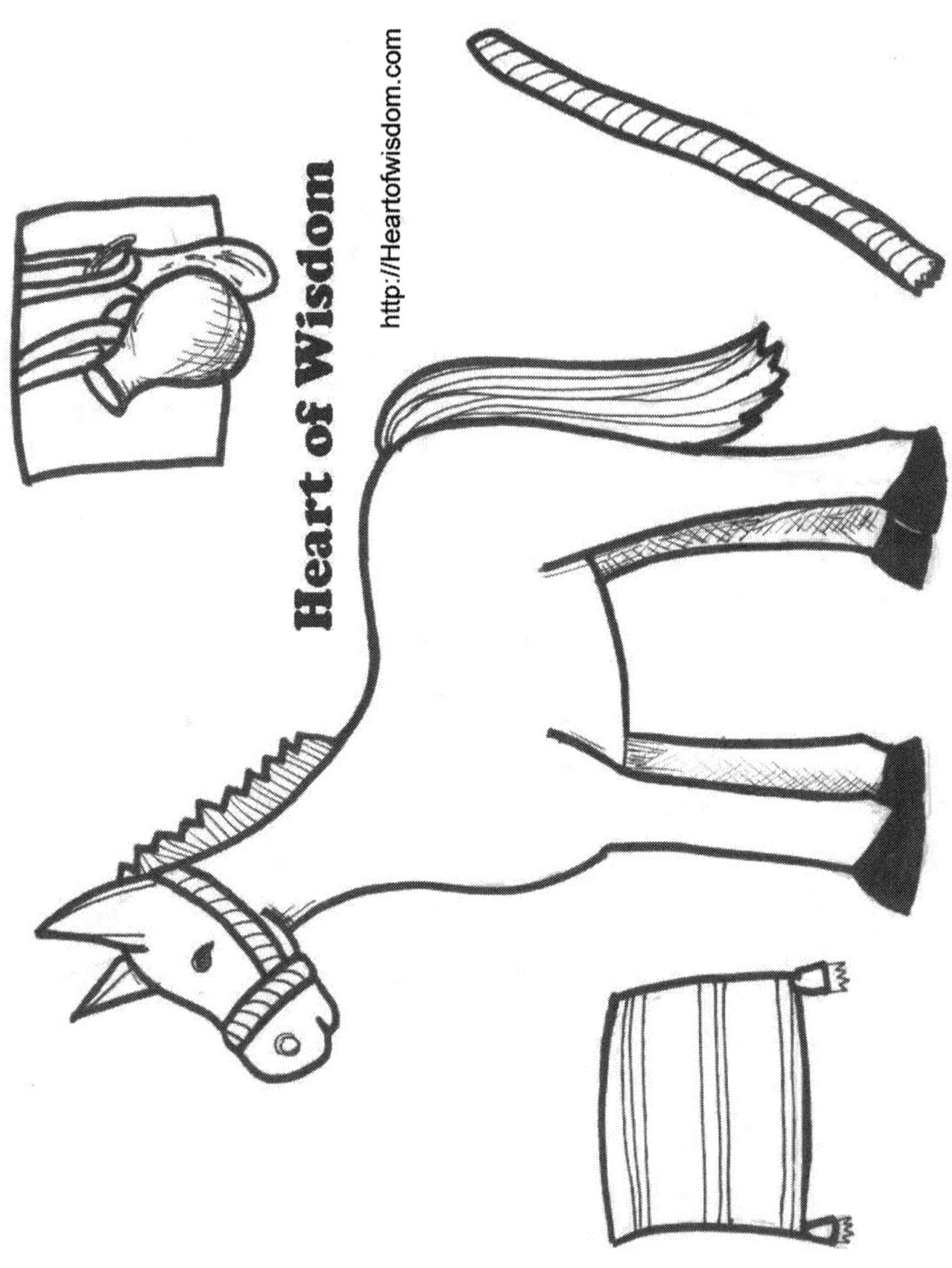

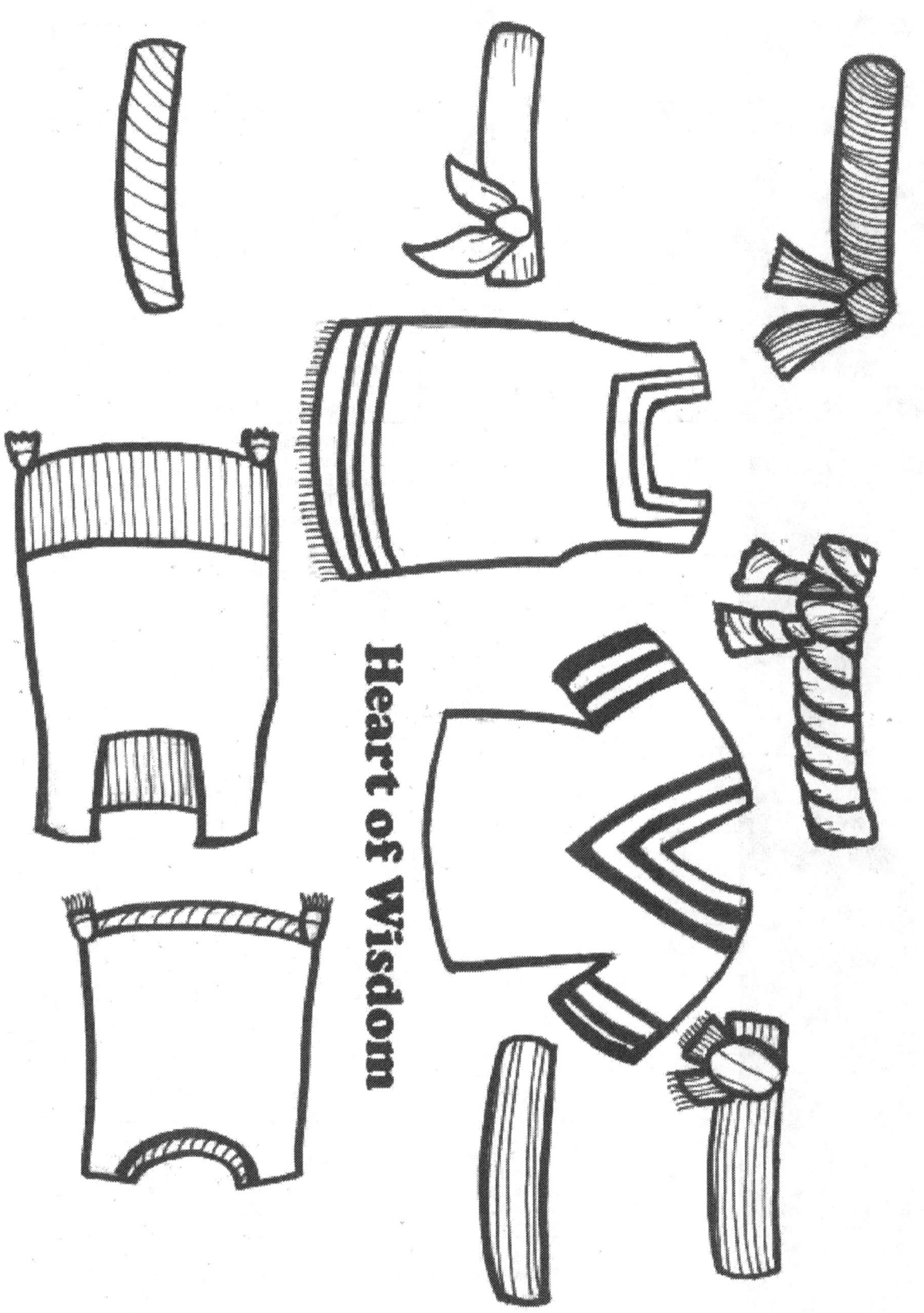

THE HEART OF WISDOM TEACHING APPROACH

COMING IN 2004
Check our Web site for publication date

The homeschool movement has brought about (or restored) many superior, efficient, and exciting teaching approaches. These methods verify that we need to renew our thinking concerning education. The Heart of Wisdom Teaching Approach is a beautiful, exciting blend and way to organize several of these excellent teaching methods. See below:

Bible First!	The Bible—the ultimate living book—is the center of education, and all subordinate studies should be brought into the circle of light radiating from the Bible. Academics play an important part, but they are secondary to the Word of God. Students spend a large portion of the school day studying God's Word, and the other half studying God's world in the light of His Word.
A Return to Biblical Hebraic Education	The Bible outlines how we should teach our children. The ancient Hebraic aim of education was ethical and religious rather than merely intellectual, and study is a form of worship. The method of instruction in the home was oral, and learning was accomplished by practice. The ancient Hebrews taught no distinction between the sacred and secular areas of life. Every detail of life must be set apart and consecrated to the glory of God.
Charlotte Mason's Philosophy	Students should develop a love of learning by reading real books—living books—as opposed to "twaddle" or "dumbed-down" literature. Each Heart of Wisdom Unit Study suggests one or more novels or biographies, but our main book is *the* living book—God's Word. Mason's method also incorporates copy work, narration (which involves the assimilating of information and, in order to retell it, the student's mind does the sorting, sequencing, selecting, connecting, rejecting and classifying), creating a Time Line Book, and developing a "Nature Diary."
The 4-Step Lessons	These four steps are a cycle of instruction loosely based on teaching to the Four Learning Styles developed by Dr. Bernice McCarthy and other learning style experts. This system is an excellent way to systematically organize the Charlotte Mason approach and the other approaches listed here.
Unit Study	The "unit" or "theme" part of the name refers to the idea of studying a topic as a whole instead of as several "subjects." A unit study takes a topic and lives with it for a period of time, integrating science, social studies, language arts, and fine arts as they apply.
Lifestyle of Learning	An approach outlined in *Wisdom's Way of Learning* by Marilyn Howshall. The emphasis is on parents relying on the Holy Spirit's guidance to provide the needed resources so that children can develop expertise in their fields of interest. Howshall explains how using these simple and natural tools (with the emphasis on the process of learning rather than the product of learning) will allow your children to begin to develop their own lifestyle of learning.
Delight-Directed Learning	Students acquire basic concepts of learning (reading, reasoning, writing, researching, etc.) during the process of examining the topic they are interested in. Education ought to be about building learners' abilities to do useful things.
Notebook or Portfolio Approach	Students think on paper—to discover connections, describe processes, express emerging understandings, raise questions, and find answers, encouraging higher-level thinking skills. This is similar to the Notebook Approach; students learn to Research, Reason, Relate, and Record. This method forces the student to internalize, learning in such a way that he/she understands better and retains the information longer.
Writing to Learn	Students create a Bible Portfolio, Unit Study Portfolio, Time Line Book, Spelling Notebook, a Vocabulary Notebook, etc. The Portfolios reflect the student's history of collecting, reading, writing and projects on specific topics as if the student were writing his or her own textbook! Each year, the Portfolios will reflect changes in the student's abilities, depth, focus, and spiritual growth.

Talk to other homeschoolers using the HOW Teaching Approach
on our Message Board at http://Heartofwisdom.com/Forum

I have been homeschooling for 10 years. My husband has been a public school teacher for 9 years. We have been in constant prayer ...we were so very excited about your curriculum, and yet, in all of my years of scouring catalogs and curriculum searches, I had never heard of you!! When I discovered you, I could not contain myself! In all my years of teaching, I have struggled through with writing/creating my own curriculum/units. It was so much work, but I never found anything out there that matched all of my philosophies/approaches to teaching and learning! You are an answer to my prayers, and I know many others'! This approach is the *best by far* that I've ever seen to help parents do that in a BIBLICAL way!!!

We have had only positive times since we started Heart of Wisdom. Our five year old is coming along in leaps and bounds with her biblical knowledge which is always encouraging to see in your children. I put this sudden growth in her down to the discussion and writing/drawing that goes on after we have read a Bible story rather than just the reading. I could go on and on about how changing to HOW and the 4 step lessons has been a positive change for our homeschool.

We are just getting started on this journey and I already love it. I am so pleased to find an Hebraic approach to learning that is for the entire family, not just the school-aged.

I am using HOW with one daughter now (age 14) and another (age 13) will soon join her. I love it. It is so versatile both in use for different ages and in activities for different learning styles, etc. It is the first Bible study plan that I have stuck with for more than a week or two. Plenty of variety in this area too, than I ever learned at school!

After reading about the Heart of Wisdom approach in *What Your Child Needs to Know When* it changed my life. We dropped everything and began one of our best years ever. We just used the Bible and other living books I had on hand, all three children (16, 11, 3) working together enjoying the Bible just from what you outlined in the book...

I have found that using HOW has developed in my daughter a love of the Bible and has made a great change in her character development...

WHAT YOUR CHILD NEEDS TO KNOW WHEN
INCLUDES EVALUATION CHECK LISTS FOR GRADES K-8

Have you ever worried if you were "doing enough"? Worry no more! Evaluate up to five children with this book! Studies show "Evaluation Check Lists" are far superior to Achievement Tests! The valuable "Evaluation Check Lists," based on National Achievement Tests, made the original *What Your Child Needs to Know When* a bestseller for the past four years. This new expanded edition includes over 200 new pages, including not only the test requirements, but also Bible reading check lists, character check lists, answers to frequently asked questions, the Greek roots of state education, education in Bible times, world views, better evaluation methods, and an introduction to *The Heart of Wisdom* teaching philosophy (reading through the Bible once a year and creating a Bible portfolio while incorporating all academic subjects)! The goals outlined in this book will help you prepare, teach, and evaluate your children from a Biblical world view. It will also advise you in helping them become self-motivated, lifelong learners. **Over 300 pages.**

A FAMILY GUIDE TO THE Biblical Holidays

WITH ACTIVITIES FOR ALL AGES

Learn the teaching method God uses to teach His children. The ultimate hands-on Bible lessons! Teach your children the way God instructed the Hebrews to teach their children—with annual events telling the story of His people and the coming of Jesus. See Jesus' death, burial, and resurrection, all foretold in the Spring holidays, and find out how to recognize His second coming by learning about the Fall holidays! This giant almost 600 page book gives an overview of nine holidays Passover, Unleavened Bread, Firstfruits, Pentecost, Trumpets, Day of Atonement, Tabernacles, Hanukkah, and Purim. This book explains the historical, agricultural, spiritual and prophetic purposes of each holiday showing how each points to Christ, and creative ways to teach them to your children! Includes projects, crafts, recipes, games, and songs for celebrating each holiday. Also includes instructions for a weekly Bible study and instructions using the Special Home School Section to incorporate the teaching of the Biblical holidays with the academic school subjects! Excellent, fascinating information about the true New Testament Church and our Hebrew Roots also included! If you only buy one book this year-make it this one! **597 Pages.**

WISDOM UNIT STUDY

Get on the Right Path, NOW!

Is your homeschooling on the right path? Are you reaching for the right goal? It does not matter how hard you try or how diligent you are if you don't have the right directions. Are you headed in the right direction? Many homeschoolers are following the wrong map on their homeschool journey. They follow the state standards, curriculum scope and sequence or SAT benchmarks. This unique unit study is a map to TRUE Wisdom. Grades 7-12.

Suppose you wanted to go to a city in Texas but you were given a map to Florida mislabeled Texas? Following the directions would not work even if you changed your tried harder, or increased your speed. You would still be lost! The problem is not your attitude or effort. The problem is you have the wrong map. Many homeschoolers are following the wrong map on their homeschool journey. They follow the state standards, curriculum scope and sequence or SAT benchmarks. This unique unit study is a map to TRUE Wisdom. **120 Pages.**

This study is one of the most important things you will ever do with your children!

COMING SOON!

Read free excerpts at Homeschool-Books.com

Several Key Resources are available from http://Homeschool-Books.com. All proceeds from the Heart of Wisdom store go to the development of Heart of Wisdom Unit Studies.

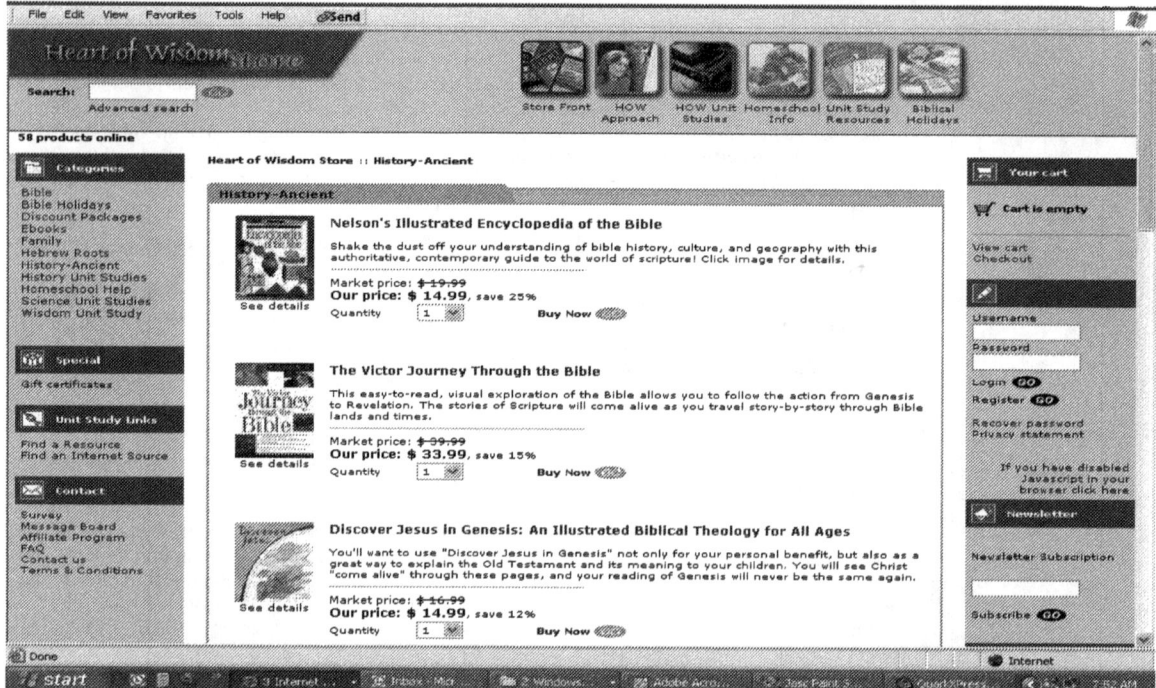

Discount Packages also available.

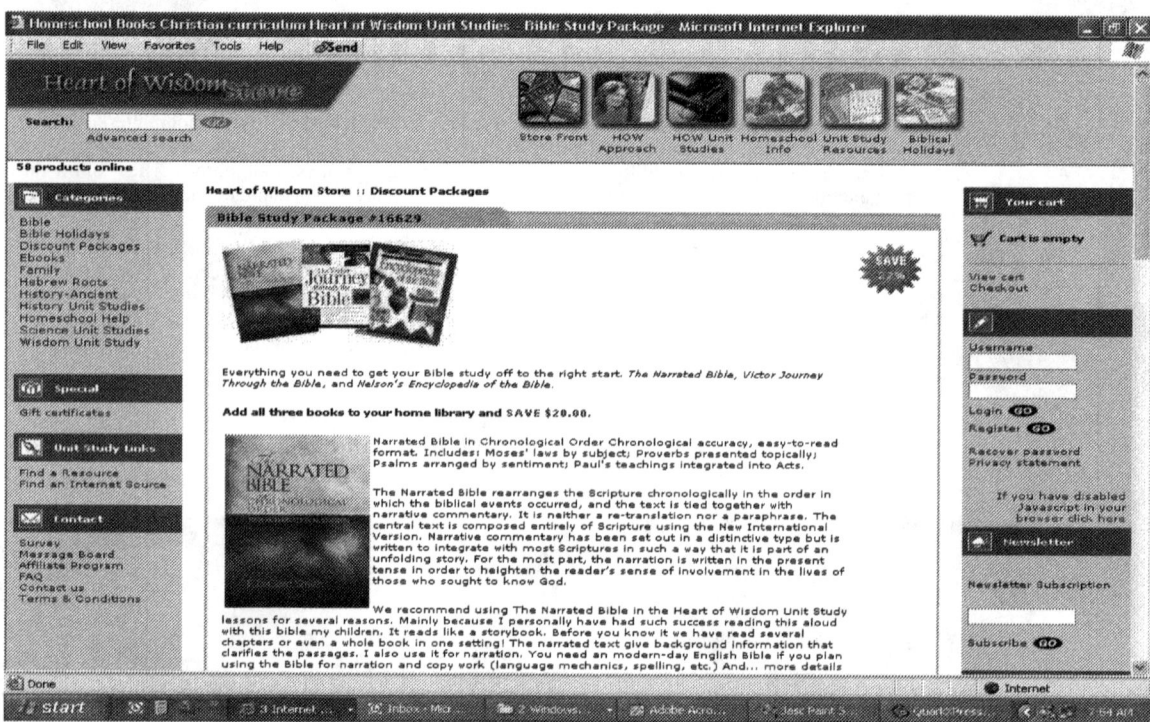

ADAM